on
cocaine

Freud
on
cocaine

'on'

'on'
Published by Hesperus Press Limited
19 Bulstrode Street, London w1u 2jn
www.hesperuspress.com

Introduction and English language translation © David Carter, 2011
This collection first published by Hesperus Press Limited, 2011

Designed and typeset by Fraser Muggeridge studio
Printed in Jordan by Jordan National Press

ISBN: 978-1-84391-601-7

Contents

Introduction

One cannot in all honesty assert that Sigmund Freud contributed directly to the invention of a world-renowned beverage, containing coca, kola nut extract and other ingredients, but his writings on the uses of the coca plant, and the alkaloid cocaine derived from it, raised hopes both in Europe and in America, that a remarkable new panacea had indeed been discovered.

The coca plant, *erythroxylon coca*, had in fact been known about since the Spanish conquest of South America, and its general effects of raising the spirits and increasing the capacity for physical work had been observed, if not understood. The cocaine alkaloid had already been isolated by the German chemist, Friedrich Gaedke, in 1855, and it was further investigated by other German scientists in the course of the nineteenth century. In 1879, at the University of Würzburg, Vassili von Anrep developed experiments with frogs to demonstrate the analgesic properties of the alkaloid.

On returning from a visit to Peru in 1859, an Italian doctor, Paolo Mantegazza, had published a report of his discovery of coca in that country, together with details of his subsequent experiments with it on himself. This work in particular was greatly respected by Freud. When, in 1884, he was reading reports of recent research in the hope of finding a field in which he might make a name for himself, he discovered that there was already considerable interest in cocaine and a body of work on it. To what extent Freud was aware of the already existing popularity of the substance in America is unclear, though it is known that he made use of the bibliography in the 'Index-catalogue' of the American Army Library. In 1863 an Italian chemist called Angelo Mariani had started marketing a wine containing an extract of coca, and the product, under the name of 'Mariani Wine', would become popular throughout Europe as well as in America. That Freud's first paper, 'On Coca', in 1884, was read in America as well as in Europe is known from Freud's account in a letter to his fiancée, Martha, on 10 February, 1886. In this he reports the enthusiasm for his paper expressed by a German scientist who had been living in America for some years and whom he had met in Paris. Thus it is safe to say at least that Freud, among others, had contributed to raising the profile of the alkaloid, when John Styth Pemberton decided, in 1886, to add a little coca leaf to his original recipe for his dark, fizzy beverage which was to conquer the world. The coca leaf extract would continue to be a crucial ingredient until the passing of the Pure Food and Drug Act of 1906. Since then coca leaves have continued to be used as flavouring but with the active ingredient removed.

One of the earliest indications of Freud's interest in the substance occurs in his letter to Martha on 21 April, 1884. Here he reports that he has ordered some to be sent to him, and he is already hoping that it might alleviate the suffering of his close friend and colleague, Ernst von Fleischl-Marxow. At the age of twenty-four, Fleischl had had the thumb of his right hand amputated, after contracting an infection. The infection persisted and he was in a constant state of pain, coping only by taking morphine, to which he became addicted. Freud endeavoured to help him overcome the addiction by the use of cocaine, but his friend eventually developed chronic cocaine intoxication. Freud thought that Fleischl would probably only live for another six months or so, but in fact his agony dragged on for many more years. It is clear that Freud suffered guilt feelings about his treatment of his friend for many years to come, especially in relation to his initial encouragement of subcutaneous injections which he later repudiated and the memory of which he appears to have repressed. This is revealed in, among other ways, the associations with coca in his accounts of some of his dreams in *The Interpretation of Dreams*, two of which, referred to as 'Irma's Injection' and 'The Botanical Monologue', are included in the present volume.

From a modern perspective it appears reckless of Freud to have experimented both on himself and on his friend, when so little was known about the effects of the alkaloid. Such practice was however common at the time. The editor of the critical edition of Freud's works on cocaine in German, Albrecht Hirschmüller, has provided convincing arguments in defence of Freud's methodology and examined claims that his essays were groundbreaking in the development of modern pharmacology (Hirschmüller, 1996). The pharmacologist, Robert Byck, made such claims, especially for the second of Freud's papers, 'A Contribution to Knowledge about the Effect of Coca' (1885), in his introduction to the English edition of the papers (Byck, 1974). Hirschmüller argues that the usual procedures in conducting research into possible new medications had already been undertaken, including experimenting on animals, and that Freud's decision to experiment on himself was the next logical step. It does seem however that Freud did not take the standard precautions, neither ensuring that antidotes were at hand nor that colleagues were nearby, etc., and was thus putting his own life at risk. His further experiments on colleagues and on himself were also conducted under conditions common at the time but which were primitive by modern standards: testing on an insufficient number of persons and with few repetitions of the same experiments, as well as failing to use any control groups. And only a matter of days after experimenting on himself he tried cocaine out on Fleischl.

It must also be admitted that in his reading on the subject Freud clearly lent greater credence to those studies which came to favourable conclusions about the applications of cocaine than to those which were sceptical. Nevertheless, Freud's studies were considered to be the best summary of the applications of cocaine for the next seventy years or so (Byck, 1974).

Another aspect of Freud's involvement with cocaine which has attracted some attention is the question of priority in the discovery of its use as a local anaesthetic. He clarified this in his letter to Fritz Wittels in 1924, in which he pointed out that it was his friend Leopold Königstein, who was most concerned about being recognised for his contribution to the research, and not Freud, who supported Karl Koller's claim to this honour all the way: 'I ascribed the honour completely to Koller alone.' In the following year, 1925, he also alluded to the matter in 'An Autobiographical Study' (*Selbstdarstellung*), in which he explains that he had to finish his essay on coca quickly in order to visit his fiancée. This explains why there are small errors and omissions in the text of Freud's essay and in his own footnotes. He left Königstein with the responsibility of testing the anaesthetising effect of cocaine on the human eye. When he returned to Vienna, he found that another friend, Koller, whom Freud has also informed about his research and theories, had conducted the relevant experiments and demonstrated the effect at a conference.

Freud's second study on coca, 'A Contribution to Knowledge about the Effect of Coca', is noteworthy for its objective measurements of the effects of cocaine, both on the physical strength of the body (by the use of a dynamometer, which he describes in the essay) and on mental reaction times (by use of the so-called *Neuramöbimeter*, also described in the essay). Such equipment was in common use for experiments in the late nineteenth century. What was new in Freud's research was the demonstration of circadian rhythms, which have been subsequently shown to be common in all forms of life. He demonstrated that there was a regular pattern of daily variations in physical reactions, and that it was possible to measure the increases in physical strength induced by cocaine and correlate them with changes in mental state.

The other essays by Freud on cocaine yield little that is new. His lecture in March, 1885, 'On the General Effect of Cocaine', is a summary of the earlier two works. And his 'Remarks on Cocaine Addiction and the Fear of Cocaine', 1887, provide no new contributions to the debate but summarise his former views and cite evidence from other researchers, specifically that provided by W.A. Hammonds.

Two other works have not been included in the present volume because of their dubious authorship. In April 1885, Freud agreed to contribute to an article comparing the cocaine produced by the American firm, Parke, Davis and Co., with that produced by the company Merck in Darmstadt, Germany. The article bore the general title 'On the Various Cocaine Preparations and their Effect' and was probably written by Hans Gutt (Hirschmüller, 1996, p. 111). Only one paragraph of scarcely more than a hundred words can be attributed with certainty to Freud. Also the short text in English, entitled 'Cocaine' (1884), was long thought to have been by Freud, but the evidence against this being the case is very strong (Hirschmüller, 1996, p. 138).

Attempts have been made to trace influences of Freud's research into the effects of cocaine on the subsequent development of the psychoanalytic theories closely associated with his name. Notable among these are Jürgen vom Scheidt's study on the possible role of Freud's experiments on himself in stimulating his interest in dream interpretation (vom Scheidt, 1973) and Peter Swales's article exploring connections between the cocaine research and the later theory of the libido (Swales, 1983). All such studies have only managed to demonstrate tenuous links however, which is scarcely surprising when it is considered that in the decade following the publication of his cocaine papers, Freud was to turn away from the treatment of mental conditions by pharmacological means to develop methods of analysis and cure along purely psychological lines. A close study of the two dream analyses included in the present volume will reveal that the associations with cocaine and his essays on it are part of the dream material in each case and do not reveal any theoretical links with the process of dream construction, the dream work, nor with the process of interpretation. In each case the dream analysis is also presented by Freud deliberately in an incomplete form. He expresses quite clearly his intention not to pursue certain lines of analysis any further. Many, including Carl Jung, criticised him for failing to follow the interpretations through, but in his defence it must be stressed that he was presenting to public view material closely related to intimate matters of his own life and of people close to him, many of whom were well-known and respected figures. His prime intention was to explain the psychoanalytic theory and practice of dream interpretation. He did not in any case believe that it was possible to provide an exhaustive analysis of any dream. Thus he also refers to both dreams in other contexts in *The Interpretation of Dreams*, and, in the case of the dream of 'The Botanical Monograph', provides further extensive analysis of some aspects, to demonstrate certain mechanisms at work in dream creation. These passages have not been included in the present volume however, because they are not directly related to the cocaine studies. There is however a clear connection made by Freud between the preference to take drugs, such as morphine and cocaine, and the frustration felt at the lack of sexual satisfaction, which can lead to the development of neuroses. I have therefore included in this volume the relevant excerpt from his study 'Sexuality in the Aetiology of the Neuroses'. The work also demonstrates clearly his turning away from pharmacology to psychology.

Finally, some account should be provided concerning the organisation of the present volume, and the sources of the texts chosen with an explanation of the conventions employed. It was decided to follow a strictly chronological sequence, presenting the letters, essays and excerpts from other works in the order in which they were written, so that the reader can trace the development of Freud's interest in cocaine. The translations are based on the German texts of the essays on coca and cocaine in the critical edition with notes and introductions by Albrecht Hirschmüller (*Schriften über Kokain*). The letters are translated from the standard German edition of Freud's letters (*Briefe, 1873–1939*, 1968), and the excerpts from *The Interpretation of Dreams* (*Die Traumdeutung*) and 'Sexuality in the Aetiology of the Neuroses' ('Die Sexualität in der Ätiologie der Neurosen'), were based on the standard German 'Student Edition' (*Studienausgabe*). Details of all works are provided in the brief bibliography at the end of this volume. Freud's own notes are provided as footnotes. His comments are translated, but the titles of the works referred to are left in the original language, except in the case of those in Russian. As he occasionally misspelled a name, got a date wrong, or omitted something important, comments or corrections by the present author are included in square brackets as are the expanded versions of titles of periodicals, where possible. The translator's notes are numbered and included as endnotes. The technical terminology used by Freud, relating to chemical, anatomical and botanical concepts, and which was in common use at the time, could not in every case be translated by pre-cise English equivalents. A compromise solution was finally decided upon, whereby archaic terms were also rendered in English by archaic terms only if it is likely that they will still be reasonably familiar to modern readers. For the sake of clarity, and to avoid any con-fusion, some terms have been rendered by their modern equi-valents. Several Latin expressions and abbreviations have been left in the forms used by Freud. One of the most frequently used Latin expressions is 'cocainum muriaticum' (sometimes written as 'cocaine muriaticum' or in abbreviated form) which is cocaine hydrochloride in modern terminology. Where it is useful endnotes have been provided for further clarification of any obscure terms.

It only remains for the translator to express the considerable debt owed to Professor Dennis Burton, who was consulted about Freud's chemical terminology, and to Alan Miles who provided second opinions on other obscurities in the original German. Needless to say, the final choices made are the re-sponsibility of the translator alone. The reader can find a more detailed account of Freud's life and of the circumstances of his interest in cocaine in a companion volume by the same author, also published by Hesperus and entitled *Brief Lives: Sigmund Freud*.

– David Carter, 2011

On Cocaine

Letters to Martha:
21 April and 19 June, 1884

Vienna, Monday, 21 April 1884. At the office of the Journal

You are amazed, I'm sure, my Darling, that I'm sitting here again, after I wrote to you from the same spot only on Saturday. This is the result of the things I neglected while I was ill, and it's really embarrassing for me. Generally things are not working out for me, for the sake of a successful practice I can't work in the laboratory, nor can I celebrate the works, from which I can indeed expect a little honour. Today I was cut to the quick when my proofs of the methodological report arrived from Leipzig. Since doing that I haven't worked on anything except two small discoveries. Otherwise I am very well however, fresh as hardly ever before, and feel really fond of you, in a way I never felt in our most beautiful days here, and if I write to you so rarely, then it is the awful conflict between doing my duty and working for the *Journal* which is responsible – even yesterday, Sunday, I was very busy. Paneth visited me today and informed me, that *perhaps* I would be called out to Schwechat to deal with a case of nervous illness. Alois Schönberg has indicated the prospect of my being made an offer of employment in Pest. These are only the first steps, which not much may come of, but they are nevertheless first steps. Frau Sch. is doing much better, and I'll be glad if no more incidents occur, so that I can release her from treatment in a week's time. I'll then send her straight off to the countryside.

There's one project and one hope that I am contemplating at the moment, which I want to tell you about; perhaps nothing further will come of it. It's a therapeutic experiment. I'm reading about cocaine, the active component in coca leaves, which many Indian tribes chew, to give themselves strength to deal with de-privations and stressful situations. A German has experimented with this material on soldiers and actually reported that it made them marvellously strong and efficient. I will have the material sent to me and experiment with it, based on obvious considerations, on heart conditions and also on cases of weakness with a nervous origin, especially on the miserable condition that occurs with morphine withdrawal (as in the case of Dr Fleischl). Perhaps many others are using it, and perhaps it will be of no use. But I don't want to give up trying it out, and, as you know, if you often try to do something and always want to do it, then eventually you'll be successful. We don't need more than one such lucky success, in order to be able to start thinking about furnishing our house. But don't get it fixed in your head, my little woman, that it will necessarily be successful this time. You know that the temperament of the researcher requires two basic qualities: being sanguine in conducting experiments and critical in one's work.

After talking away about everything concerning myself, I come to you, my dear little girl. No, I'm still here, I can't think of seeing you in the spring, I would like to have done something fine before we meet again. And I'm looking forward to that enormously. I am expecting the newspaper deliverer to come today with the parcel and the money. It's true that it seems he won't come, but your visiting cards and your seal won't be long in coming anyway. It's nice that you want something for yourself, and it pleases me very much that you go for walks in the little wood. Do you go alone, my dear little Martha? Dolfi said yesterday that it would be very nice, if you could say some time, and say it proudly of course: 'I waited four years for my husband.' By the way, Martha, what do you think of the fact that little Pauli has already found happiness in love? With the twenty-eight-year-old brother of her friend, Fräulein Glaser, with whom she usually spends special holidays. He's a doctor of law and an articled clerk in a lawyer's office in our town of Neutitschein in Moravia. So he's already a person of some seriousness. What do you think of that? Don't mention it to anyone, and I don't want to say yet that the little one is definitely given away, but doesn't it look as though the silly girls will all quickly be gone, 'like hot cakes'? Dolfi is the only one who is still free, and she said yesterday – I had invited her to afternoon tea to repair my black coat – 'It must be marvellous to be the bride of an educated man, but an educated man won't have me, don't you think?' I couldn't help laughing greatly at this perception of herself.

My dear little Martha, the newspaper deliverer has just come. He brought only a few fine things, but there was a letter with twenty-eight guilders. How great it is, when a person has some money. Now, my dear, you will get ten more guilders from me. I'll keep them for a little while, because I don't have any other money, but they belong to you. What do you still need for your stock of clothes? Are Jersey cardigans still fashionable?

I'll keep the money for a while, not because I am miserly, but because the cocaine will cost me some money and because yesterday, when I had to pay out ten guilders for a piece of electrical apparatus, I made myself poor.

Now we've got all the pieces of apparatus together, and to-morrow we will begin our work. I only go to see Frau Sch. once a day however. Schönberg is struggling with Kant and Horace, but looks well and is in good spirits. My dear Martha, don't you think this all bodes well for the second book?

So, come on, write as much to me about yourself, as I am writing about myself. And also tell me whether you are very well, indeed completely well, whether the iron medicine is doing you well and whether you are drinking any wine. I'll be angry if you are not doing both.

You wanted to go back to many things in one of my recent letters. What were they then?

With warm regards

Your Sigmund

Vienna, Thursday, 19 June 1884

My Darling,

I can't remember having been in such a rush, otherwise I would have answered all your dear good little letters with long sheets full of discussions, but today I also have to make it brief. I hope we'll certainly be able to chat together soon.

The cocaine work was not finished until last night. The first half has already been corrected today, and will be one and a half pages thick. The few guilders, which I have earned from doing it, I had to deduct from the money lost, by having chased away my student today and yesterday. Now I've got the proofreading of a second work in front of me, I also have to carry out some electrical treatment, and carry out my duties for the *Journal*, but I am as healthy as a lion, cheerful and happy, and you can imagine that this is not a mood in which I want to drop everything and become an attendant for a mental patient.

My dear girl, you must banish completely from your mind those gloomy thoughts, such as thinking that you are standing in the way of my work. You know that the key to understanding my life is that I can only work, when spurred on by great hopes for things which dominate me completely. I was completely weary of life before I had you, and now that I have you, 'in principle', possessing you completely has become generally a requirement I impose on life, which provides me with little other pleasure. I am very defiant and reckless, and need great incentives. I have done a whole lot of things which all prudent people must consider very foolish. For example going in for science when you are very poor, and winning the heart of a poor girl when you are a very poor man. I must go on living in this fashion, risking a lot, hoping a lot, and working a lot. I've long been a lost cause for normal middle-class prudence. And now I shan't see you, or will see you only in three months, in our uncertain circumstances, and with such unpredictable people as those in our family. In three months Eli could be in Hamburg, and the situation of my own people could make it impossible for me to travel. In short, I don't know what the future will bring. I can't rely on anything, but I know that I need to be revitalised by holding you in my arms again as urgently as I need food and drink. I know that I have burdened you with enough trouble and sacrifice, not to deprive you of a few weeks of being happy together, although you yourself would willingly do without it. I'll follow my own impulse, and continue to take a risk. I'll fortify myself with thoughts of you and continue, with renewed strength, to attempt to raise my spirits, and not tear myself away from all kinds of work for three months. The profit won't be a great one. What money is saved will be forfeited in the form of time, and not much money will be saved. Can you imagine that I would have a thousand guilders stowed away and let Rosa and Dolfi go hungry?

I would give them at least half of it, and what is left would be sufficient for that period, in which I could make up for what's lost. I won't be doing right by them, but I'll be doing what is right in terms of my own nature and our circumstances. I feel at one with myself about this. Today Paneth was here, and of course he was totally convinced that it was necessary that I should accept the post, but I have the good quality of having faith in myself. I have also come across many people, who admit that I'm right. But I know that I will see you again, my Dear. Keep healthy. I must finish here, because some more proofreading has arrived.

Your Sigmund

On Coca, 1884

I. The Coca Plant

The coca plant, *erythroxylon coca*, is a four to six foot high shrub, similar to our blackthorn, which is cultivated extensively in South America, especially in Peru and Bolivia. It flourishes best in the warm valleys on the eastern slopes of the Andes, at 5,000 to 6,000 English feet above sea level, in a climate with high rainfall but free of extreme temperatures.[*] The leaves, which serve as an indispensable stimulant for about ten million people,[†] are 'round like an egg, five to six cm long, petiolated, have a whole rim, with edging, and are distinguished by two creases in the form of lines which stand out especially on the underside, and which, like nerve branches, accompany the median veins from the base of the leaf to its point in a flat curve.'[‡] The shrub bears small white flowers in twos and threes in tufts on the sides and egg-shaped red fruit. It is planted as seeds or cuttings; the young plants are transplanted after one year and provide the first harvest of leaves after eighteen months. The leaves are considered to be mature, when they have become so stiff that their stems break off when you touch them. They are then dried quickly in the sun or with the aid of a fire and sewn up in sacks (*cestos*) to be transported. A coca shrub provides, in favourable circumstances, four to five harvests of leaves every year and remains fertile for thirty to forty years. With such a large yield (allegedly thirty million pounds a year), coca leaves are an important item of trade and source of taxation for those countries.[§]

[*] O.R. Markham, *Peruvian Barks* [Bark], London 1880.
[†] According to Bibra's assessment. 'Die Narkotischen Genussmittel', 1855.
[‡] For this description I have to thank Prof. Vogel in Vienna, who very kindly put his notes and books on coca at my disposal.
[§] Weddell, *Voyage dans le Nord de la Bolivie*, 1853.

II. History and Use in the Country

When the Spanish conquerors forced their way into Peru, they found that the coca plant was being cultivated in that country and was held in high regard, and was even used in close conjunction with the religious customs of the country. Legend has it that Manco Capac, the divine son of the Sun, had, in primeval times, come down from the crags of Lake Titicaca and brought his father's light to the wretched inhabitants, and had given them knowledge possessed by the gods, the ability to employ useful skills and the gift of coca, that divine plant, which satisfies the hungry, strengthens the weak and causes them to forget their bad fortune.* Coca leaves were presented as offerings to the gods and they were chewed while performing religious practices, and they were even put into the mouths of the dead, to assure them of a favourable reception in the other world. As the chronicler of the Spanish conquest,[†] himself a descendant of the Incas, reports, coca was at first scarce in the country and its consumption the prerogative of the rulers. At the time of the conquest however it had already been available to everyone for a long time. Garcilasso endeavoured to defend coca against the ban which the conquerors had imposed on it. The Spaniards did not believe in the marvellous effects of the plant, which because of its role in the religious ceremonies of the conquered people they suspected of being the devil's work. A council in Lima even forbad its consumption for being heathen and sinful. But they changed their attitude when they noticed that the Indians could not accomplish the heavy work imposed on them in the mines, if the consumption of coca was denied them. They settled for distributing coca leaves to the workers three or four times a day and allowing them short rest periods, so that

* Scrivener, 'On the coca leaf and its uses in diet and medicine', *Medical Times and Gazette*, 1871 [vol 2, p. 407 et seq.]
† Garcilasso de la Vega, *Comentariós reales de los Incas, 1609–17.*

they could chew their beloved coca leaves. Thus coca has retained its standing among the natives up to the present day. Traces of the religious veneration with which it was held can still be found.[*]

An Indian always carries with him on his travels a pouch containing coca leaves (called a *chuspa*) and also a flask of the ashes of the plant (*llicta*).[†] He forms a bite-size piece (*acullico*) of the leaves in his mouth, pierces it several times with a thorn dipped in the ashes[‡] and chews it slowly and thoroughly with substantial secretion of saliva. In other areas a kind of earth, called *tonra*, is said to be added to the leaves instead of ashes of the plant. Chewing three or four ounces of the leaves daily is not considered immoderate. According to Mantegazza, Indians start using this stimulant in early youth and continue with it till the end of their lives. Whenever they have an exhausting journey to go on, or whenever they make love to a woman, and generally whenever a greater demand is made on their strength, they increase the usual dose.

What purpose it is intended to achieve by the addition of the alkaline salts in the ashes, is unclear. Mantegazza reports that he had chewed coca leaves with and without *llicta* and felt no difference. According to Martius[§] and Demarle,[¶] the cocaine, which is probably contained in a compound with coca tannin, is released by the alkaline salts of the plant ashes. A *llicta* analysed by Bibra consisted of 29% calcium carbonate and magnesia, 34% potash, 3% alumina and iron, insoluble compounds of alumina, silica, and 17% iron, 5% carbon and 10% water.

A wealth of evidence is available showing that under the influence of coca Indians can bear exceptional strain and

[*] Christison, 'Observations on the effect[s] of cuca, or coca, the leaves of *erythroxylon coca*'. *British Medical Journal*, 1876.
[†] Mantegazza, 'Sulle virtù igieniche e medicinali della coca', Milan, 1859.
[‡] Scrivener loc cit.
[§] *Systema mat. med.* [*Systema materiae medicae vegetabilis brasiliensis*] Brasil.
[¶] 'Essai sur la coca du Pérou', Thèse de Paris, 1862.

accomplish heavy work, without needing any actual nourishment while doing it.* Valdos y Palacios[†] reports that with the aid of coca Indians can go on foot for hundreds of hours, and what is more can run faster than horses, without showing any signs of fatigue. Castelnau,[‡] Martius,[§] and Scrivener[¶] all confirm this, and Humboldt talks of it in his journey to the equinoctial regions as a universally known fact. The reports by Tschudi[‖] about the achievements of a *cholos* (person of mixed race), whom he was able to observe closely, are much quoted. The man carried out laborious excavations for him for five days and five nights, without sleeping more than two hours every night and without consuming anything but coca. After the work was finished he accompanied him during a two-day ride, running alongside his mule. He assured him that he would willingly carry out the same work again without eating, if he was given enough coca. The man was sixty-two years old and had never been ill.

In *The Journey of the Frigate Novara* there are reports of similar examples of heightened capability through the use of coca. Weddell,[**] von Meyen,[††] Markham,[‡‡] and even Poeppig,[§§] who is the source of much malicious gossip about coca, can only confirm this effect of coca, which since it has become well known, has not ceased to arouse the astonishment of the world.

---

* Compare Fronmüller, 'Coca und Cat. [Pharmakologische Studien]',
Prager Vierteljahrschrift für praktische Heilkunde, Vol 79, 1863.
† *Viagem da cidade de Cuzco a de Belem*, 1840 [Valdez e Palacios]
‡ *Expédition dans les parties centrals de l'Amérique du Sud*, 1851 [vol 4, 1852].
§ *Reise in Brasilien von Spix und Martius*, 1831.
¶ Loc cit.
‖ *Reiseskizzen aus Peru in den Jahren 1838 und 1842* [Peru. Reiseskizzen aus den Jahren 1838–42, 1846].
** Loc cit.
†† *Reise um die Welt* [Reise um die Erde].
‡‡ *Travels in Peru and India*, 1862.
§§ *Reise in Chili* [Chile], *Peru und auf dem Amazonenstrom*, 1827–32.

Other reports stress the ability of the *coqueros* (coca-chewers) to tolerate a longer period of doing without food without any trouble. According to Unanuè,* only those inhabitants of the city of La Paz who had consumed coca could stay alive during the famine, when it was besieged in 1781. According to Stevenson,[†] the inhabitants of several areas of Peru often refrain from all forms of nourishment for days on end by using coca, without interrupting their work.

According to all this evidence and considering the role which coca has played for centuries in South America, one may reject the view sometimes expressed, that the effect of coca is an imaginary one and that the natives are able to accomplish the achievements mentioned without it by force of circumstances and by practice. One should expect to hear however, that the *coqueros* make up for it during their periods of rest through an increased intake of nourishment, or that their lifestyle leads them into rapid decline. The former does not follow definitely from the travellers' reports; and the latter behaviour is contradicted most firmly by trustworthy witnesses. It is true that Poeppig has drawn a repulsive picture of the physical and intellectual decadence, which is said to be the inevitable consequence of habitual coca consumption, but all other observers express the view that the moderate consumption of cocaine is beneficial rather than harmful to health and point out that the *coqueros* live to a ripe old age.[‡] Excessive use of coca certainly produces, according to Weddell and Mantegazza, cachexia, which manifests itself physically in problems with digestion, loss of weight and suchlike, and mentally in ethical decline and complete apathy towards everything, which is not related to consumption of the stimulant. White people also sometimes

* 'Disertacion sobre el aspecto, cultivo, comercio y virtudes de la famosa planta del Peru nombrada Coca', Lima, 1794.
† [Stevenson] *Historical and descriptive narrative of twenty years residence in South America*, 1825.
‡ Fronmüller loc cit.

succumb to this condition, which reveals much similarity with the manifestations of chronic alcoholism and morphine addiction. It is notable, that cachexia caused by coca is only induced among the *coqueros* by the toxic effect of the excessive consumption of coca and never by a possible disparity between the intake of nourishment and the work accomplished.

III. Coca Leaves in Europe – Cocaine

The oldest recommendation for the use of coca is, according to Dowdeswell,* included in a paper by Dr Monardes (Seville, 1569), which appeared in an English translation in 1569. Like the later reports of the Jesuit priest Padre Antonio Julian† and the doctor Pedro Crespo, both in Lima, it praises the effect of the plant against hunger and tiredness. The latter two authors had great hopes for the introduction of coca into Europe. In 1749 the plant was brought to Europe and described by A.L. de Jussieu and designated as belonging to the genus *erythroxylon*, and then included by Lamarck in his *Encyclopédie Méthodique Botanique* of 1876. Reports of travellers, such as Tschudi, Markham and others provided the proof, that the effect of coca leaves was not restricted to the Indian race.

In 1859 Paolo Mantegazza, who had lived for a number of years in the coca countries of South America, published his experiences of the physiological and therapeutic effect of coca leaves‡ in both hemispheres. Mantegazza praises coca enthusiastically and provided evidence in the case histories he included

* 'The coca leaf', *The Lancet*, 1876.
† 'Disertacion sobre Hayo ó Coca', Lima, 1787 [it is actually a chapter title in *La perla de la América*].
‡ 'Sulle virtù igieniche e medicinali della coca'. Memoria onorata del Premio dell'Acqua nel concorsodi di 1858, estratta dagli *Annali Universali di Medicina*, 1859. There is a short report on it in the *Österreichische Zeitschrift für praktische Heilkunde* in the same year.

for its versatile therapeutic use. His report aroused a lot of attention but few trusted it. I have encountered so many correct observations in Mantegazza's work, that I am inclined to accept the validity of those pieces of information which I did not have the opportunity to confirm.

In the year 1859 Dr Scherzer, a member of the expedition by the Austrian frigate *Novara*, brought some coca leaves to Vienna, a part of which he sent to be examined by Prof. Wöhler. From them Wöhler's student Niemann* produced an alkaloid, cocaine. Another student of Wöhler's, Lossen,[†] continued after Niemann's death with the investigation into the elements contained in the coca leaves. The cocaine (Niemann's) crystalises in large four- to six-sided prisms of the clinorhombic system. It tastes bitter and causes anaesthesia in the mucous membranes. It softens at ninety-eight degrees and is difficult to dissolve in water, but easily soluble in alcohol, ether and diluted acids. It provides double salts with platinum chloride and gold chloride. When heated with hydrochloric acid it breaks down into benzoic acid, methyl alcohol and a base which has been little studied: *ecgonine*. The chloride and the acetate are suitable for physiological and therapeutic use due to the fact that they are easily soluble in water.[‡]

Apart from cocaine the following are also found in coca leaves: coca tannin, a strange wax, and a volatile base, hygrine, the smell of which is reminiscent of trimethylamine, and which Lossen obtained in the form of a viscous, bright yellow oil. According to some indications in the reports by chemists, the series of new substances contained in coca leaves does not appear to be exhausted yet.

* *Annal. d. Chemie u. Pharmac.* 114 and *Vierteljahrsschrift für praktische Pharmacie*, 9.
† *Annalen der Chemie und Pharmacie* 133.
‡ Husemann and Hilger, *Die Pflanzenstoffe etc.* – Girtler, *Über Coca, Extractum der Coca und Cocain. Wiener med.Wochenschrift* [*Wiener medicinische Wochenschrift*] *1862.*

Since the discovery of cocaine numerous observers have examined the effect of coca on animals, and healthy and sick human beings, partly using a preparation called cocaine, and partly an infusion of coca leaves, or the method used by the Indians. In Austria Schroff, the elder, carried out the first experiments on animals, and other reports on coca have been produced by Frankl (1860), Fronmüller (1863) and Neudörfer (1870). In Germany one must record the recommendation as therapy by Clemens (1867), the animal experiments by von Anrep (1880) and the experiments by Aschenbrandt on exhausted soldiers (1883).

In England A. Bennett carried out the first experiments on animals in 1874; a sensation was created in 1876 by the reports of the aged President of the British Medical Association, Sir Robert Christison; and when a correspondent of the *British Medical Journal* put forward the claim that Mr Weston, who astonished the scientific world of London with his achievements as a walker, was chewing coca leaves, coca had become an object of general interest for some time. In the same year (1876) Dowdeswell published a report on a thoroughly inconclusive experimental investigation in the physiological laboratory of University College, since when coca seems not to have attracted any investigators in England.

In the French literature on the subject the following should be mentioned: Rossier (1861), Demarle (1862), Gosse's monograph on *erythroxylon coca* (1862), Reiss (1866), Lippmann, *Étude sur la coca du Pérou* (1868), Moréno y Maïz (1868), who provided a new description of cocaine, Gazeau (1870), Collin (1877) and Marvaud in his book *Les Aliments d'épargne* (1874), which is the only one of the works mentioned which was at my disposal.

In Russia Nikolsky, Danini (1873) and Tarhanoff (1872) especially have studied the effect of cocaine on animals; numerous reports on the successful therapeutic use of coca preparations have come from North America in recent years, which have all been reviewed in the *Detroit Therapeutic Gazette*.

The effect of the older of the works cited here was, on the whole, to evoke great disappointment and the conviction that effects, such as those coca was credited with in South America, could not be expected in Europe. Investigations such as those by Schroff, Fronmüller and Dowdeswell provided negative or not very remarkable results. For these failures more than one explanation presents itself. Above all the quality of the preparations used is probably to blame.* Several authors themselves express doubts on the quality of their preparations, and, insofar as they believe the reports of the travellers about the effect of coca, they assume that this can be attributed to a volatile component of the leaf. And in doing so they refer to the information provided by Poeppig and others, that in South America leaves which had been stored for a considerable time were also considered useless. Only the experiments which were conducted recently using the cocaine produced by Merck in Darmstadt justify the assertion that cocaine is the actual carrier of the coca effect, which can be elicited just as well in Europe as in South America and can be utilised in dietetic and therapeutic ways.

IV. The Effect of Coca on Animals

As we know that animals of different genera – and even individuals within the same genus – do not differ from each other very much, except in those chemical peculiarities which determine their receptivity to substances which are foreign to the organism, we cannot, from the outset, expect to find again something in the effect of coca on animals which is similar to the effect as described of coca leaves on human beings. It can be

---

* The cocaine content of the coca leaves fluctuates, according to Lossen, between 0.2% and 0.02%. 0.05 grains of *cocaine muriaticum* seems to be the effective dose for human beings. A dried coca leaf weighs one decigram according to Lippmann ('Étude sur la coca du Péru'. Thèse de Strasbourg, 1868).

considered a satisfactory result if we are able to understand both kinds of effect from identical perspectives.

We have to thank von Anrep[*] for the most detailed experiments on the effect of coca on animals. Before him such experiments have been carried out by Schroff, the elder,[†] Moréno y Maïz,[‡] Tarhanov,[§] Nikolsky,[¶] Danini,[||] A. Bennett[**] and Ott.[††] The majority of these authors have applied the alkaloid internally or through subcutaneous absorption.

The most common result of these investigations is that the cocaine has a stimulating effect on the nervous system in smaller doses and a paralysing effect in larger doses. The numbing effect is particularly noticeable in the poisoning of cold-blooded animals, while symptoms of stimulation are more prominent in warm-blooded ones.

According to Schroff, cocaine produces in frogs a soporific condition with paralysis of the voluntary muscles. Moréno y Maïz, Danini, Nikolsky and Ott have found essentially the same effects. Moréno y Maïz reports that with doses which are not too large tetanus precedes the general paralysis. With the same conditions Nikolsky describes a stage of excitement of the musculature, but Danini on the other hand has never observed any spasms.

Also, according to von Anrep, cocaine has a paralysing effect on frogs after a short period of excitement. To be precise first

[*] 'Über die physiologische Wirkung des Cocains'. *Pflügers Archiv*, XXI, 1880.
[†] 'Vorläufige Mitteilung[en] über Cocain.' *Wochenblatt der Gesellschaft der Ärzte in Wien*, 1862.
[‡] *Recherches chimiques et physiologiques sur l'erythroxylon coca du Pérou*, 1868.
[§] *Cocaine and Diabetes*, 1872 [Russian].
[¶] 'Article on the effect of cocaine on animal organisms' [Russian].
[||] 'On the physiological effect and therapeutic application of cocaine', 1872 [1873] [Russian].
[**] 'An experimental inquiry into the physiological action of theine etc [of theine, caffeine, guaranine, cocaine and theobromine].' *Edinburgh Medical and Surgical Journal*, 1874 [1873].
[††] 'Coca and its alkaloid cocain[e].' *New York Medical Record*, 1876.

the sensitive nerve endings and then the sensitive nerves themselves are impaired, and then respiration is at first accelerated and then brought to a stop, and heart activity is slowed down till the diastolic action stops. Doses of two milligrams are enough to bring about symptoms of poisoning.

According to Schroff's experiments on rabbits, the details of which are marked by inconsistencies, cocaine causes in them many different kinds of spasm, an increase in the breathing and pulse rates, dilation of the pupils and death accompanied by convulsions. The success of the poisoning depended to a large extent on the nature of the application. According to Danini, cocaine poisoning in warm-blooded creatures causes first excitement, which expresses itself in continuous jumping and running, then in paralysis of muscular activity, and finally in clonic spasms. Tarhanov found that after administering coca to dogs there was an increase in mucus secretion and sugar in the urine.

In the experiments by von Anrep the effect of cocaine, up to high doses, on warm-blooded creatures revealed itself in animated excitement first of the psyche[1] and then of the brain centres controlling voluntary movement. On absorption of 0.01 grams of cocaine per kilo dogs show obvious signs of the most joyful excitement and a maniacal urge to move around. Von Anrep sees indications in the character of these movements that all the nerve centres are in the grip of this excitement, and he also interprets certain oscillating movements of the head as symptoms of stimulation of the semicircular canals. Further characteristics of cocaine intoxication are: an increase in the frequency of respiration, a rapid acceleration of the pulse rate caused by premature paralysis of the n. vagi, dilation of the pupils, increased bowel activities, a great increase in blood pressure and reduction in secretions. The muscular material which lies crosswise remains intact even with large doses, which finally lead to spasms, symptoms of paralysis and death through paralysis of the respiratory tract. Von Anrep did not determine the lethal dose for dogs, but for rabbits it amounts to 0.10 grams and for cats 0.02 grams per kilo.*

After detaching the spinal cord from the oblongata, cocaine produces neither spasms nor a rise in blood pressure (Danini); after severing the pectoral medulla, cocaine spasms occur in the front extremities but not in the rear ones (von Anrep). Danini and von Anrep therefore assume that the effect of the cocaine is directed above all at the vital area of the medulla oblongata.

It should also be mentioned that only Schroff, the elder, calls cocaine a narcotic and aligns it with opium and cannabis, while almost all other researchers rank it with caffeine.

V. The Effect of Coca on Healthy Humans

I have been able to study the effect that the taking of cocaine has on the healthy human organism, in repeated experiments on myself and others, and I have found it to be essentially in accordance with Mantegazza's account of the effect of coca leaves.†

On the first occasion I took 0.05 grams of cocaine muriaticum in a 1% aqueous solution, in a slightly bad mood brought about by tiredness. This solution is quite viscous, somewhat opalescent, with a strange aromatic smell. It arouses what is at first the sensation of a bitter taste, which then turns into a sequence of very pleasant aromatic sensations. Dry cocaine hydrochloride produces the same smell and taste to a larger extent.

---

* By subcutaneous injection.
† I used, as did Aschenbrandt (*Deutsche medicin. Wochenschrift Dez* 1883 [*Deutche medicinische Wochenschrift Dezember 1883*]), the cocaine hydrochloride produced by Merck in Darmstadt. It can be bought in Haubner's pharmacy, the Engelapotheke am Hof, at a price, which is not much higher than that of Merck, but which must still be described as a very high one. The management of the pharmacy has kindly announced that they are endeavouring to lower the price of the substance by establishing links with other sources of supply.

A few minutes after taking it one suddenly becomes more cheerful and a feeling of lightness occurs. One feels at the same time some furriness on the lips and palate, and then a sense of warmth in the same places, and if one then drinks cold water, one experiences it as warm on the lips but as cold at the back of the throat. On other occasions a pleasant coolness prevails in the mouth and in the throat.

In the first experiment there occurred a short stage with toxic effects, which I noticed were absent later. Breathing became lower and deeper, and I felt weak and sleepy, had to yawn frequently and found myself in considerable high spirits. After a few minutes the real state of cocaine euphoria began, introduced by a repeated belching, which had a cooling effect. Immediately after taking the cocaine I noticed a slight slowing down of my pulse rate, and then a moderate increase later.

I have observed the same indications of being under the influence of cocaine in others, mainly people of the same age. The most constant proved to be the repeated belching with cooling effect. At the same time one often hears a purring sound which must occur high up in the intestine, and two of the people whom I observed, and who claimed that they were able to identify the movements of their stomachs, stated categorically, that they had experienced these effects repeatedly. Often an intensive feeling of heat as the cocaine began to take effect was reported to me, which I also felt in a few later experiments, but which were absent on other occasions. On only two occasions did the cocaine bring about a feeling of dizziness. On the whole the toxic effects of consuming cocaine are of only short duration, less intensive than those caused by effective doses of quinine or sodium salicylate, and seem to become weaker with repeated use of cocaine.

Mantegazza cites the following as occasional effects of cocaine: brief erythema, an increase in the amount of urine, dryness of the conjunctiva and the nasal mucous membrane. The dryness of the oral mucous membrane and the pharynx is a constant symptom and lasts for several hours. A slight laxative effect was reported by some observers (Marvaud, Collan*). Urine and faeces are said to acquire the smell of coca. The effect on the pulse rate is depicted by different observers in various ways. According to Mantegazza, coca very soon causes a significant increase in the pulse rate, which continues to rise with higher doses, and Collin[†] also observed a quickening of the pulse rate after taking coca, while Rossier,[‡] Demarle[§] and Marvaud noticed that after the initial quickening there followed a slowing down over a long period. Christison observed in himself that, after taking coca, physical work caused a slower rate of quickening than usual; and Reiss[¶] denied any influence on the pulse rate. I find no difficulty in explaining this lack of agreement partly by the differences between the preparations used (warm infusion of the leaves, cold cocaine solution, etc.) and the method of application, and partly by the variety of individual reactions. As Mantegazza has already reported, the latter must generally be taken into account to a large extent with coca. There are said to be people who cannot tolerate coca at all, and on the other hand I have found quite a few people, on whom the dose of five centigrams, which is effective on me and others, had no effect.

The psychic effect of *cocainum muriaticum* in doses of 0.05–0.10 grams consists in a general raising of the spirits and constant euphoria, which differs in no way from the normal euphoria of healthy human beings. The feeling of a change in condition, which accompanies the raising of spirits through alcohol, is completely lacking, as is the urge, characteristic of

* *Finska läkaresällsk. Handl.* [*Finska läkaresällskepts handlingar*] XX, 1878.
† 'De la coca et de ses [et ses] véritables propriétés thérapeutiques.' *L'Union médicale*, 1877.
‡ 'Sur l'action physiologique des feuilles de coca.' *Echo medical Suisse*, 1861.
§ 'Essai sur la coca du Pérou'. Thèse de Paris, 1862.
¶ [Reis] 'Note sur l'emploi de la coca.' *Bulletin de thérapeutique* [*Bulletin général de thérapeutique médicine*, *1886*] 1866.

the effect of alcohol, to immediate activity. One feels an increase in self-control, and feels revitalised and better able to work, but when one works the high level of excitation and heightening of intellectual powers caused by alcohol, tea or coffee is absent. One feels simply normal and soon finds it difficult to believe that one is under the influence of anything.*

One has the general impression that the mood created by cocaine in such doses has been caused not so much by direct excitation as by the absence of depressing elements in the general state of feeling. One may perhaps be permitted to assume, that the euphoria which occurs in a state of health is nothing other than the normal mood of a well-nourished cerebral cortex, which is 'unaware' of its bodily organs.

During this condition induced by cocaine, which has not been described in any greater detail, there emerges what has been described as the remarkable stimulating effect of coca. Long-lasting and intensive intellectual and muscular work is accomplished without fatigue, and the needs of nourishment and sleep, which would have otherwise imposed their demands at certain times of the day, have simply been dispelled. Under the influence of cocaine, one can, if called upon, eat a substantial amount without any aversion, but one has the distinct feeling that one had no need of the meal. Similarly, when the effect of the cocaine is wearing off, one can fall asleep if one goes to bed, but one also has no trouble in doing without sleep. In the first hours under the effect of cocaine one cannot fall asleep, but there is nothing unpleasant about this sleeplessness.

I have tested on myself about a dozen times this effect of coca in staving off hunger, sleep and tiredness and in strengthening one's ability for intellectual work; I had no opportunity to test its effect on accomplishing physical work.

* The best confirmation of the observations I made on myself are those by Wilder on himself (*Detroit Therapeutic Gazette*, Nov. 1882).

I was able to observe a striking example of neutralising extreme tiredness and a legitimate feeling of hunger in a very busy colleague, who had been sober since early morning and after concentrated activity, took 0.05 grams *cocainum muriaticum* at six o'clock in the evening. A few minutes later, he declared that he felt as though he had just risen from a sumptuous dining table, did not want to have an evening meal and considered himself to be strong enough to go for a long walk.

This stimulating effect of coca has been proven unquestionably by a series of reliable reports, including some during recent years.

The seventy-eight-year-old Sir Robert Christison[*] tired himself out to the point of exhaustion for the purposes of experiment by walking for fifteen English miles, without taking any nourishment. He repeated this after a few days with the same result. During the third experiment he chewed two drachmas of coca leaves, covered the same distance without any trouble, and felt, on arriving back home, neither hunger nor thirst in spite of his nine hour period of abstinence. And he woke up the next morning without any feeling of tiredness. On another occasion he climbed a 3,000-foot mountain, arriving at the peak completely exhausted; under the influence of coca he was able to make the descent feeling as fresh as a young man and without any fatigue.

Clemens[†] and J. Collan[‡] have experienced similar effects on themselves, the latter during long walks of several hours across snow; Mason[§] calls coca 'an excellent thing… for a long

[*] 'Observations on the effect[s] of cuca, or coca etc.' *British Medical Journal*, 1876.
[†] 'Erfahrungen über die therap. Verwendung der Cocablätter.' *Deutsche Klinik*, 1867.
[‡] J. Collan, *finska läkaresällsk. Handl.* [*Finska läkaresällskapets handlingar*] XX, 1878, according to *Schmidt's Jahrbücher*, 87 [187].
[§] 'Erythroxylon Coca; its physiological effects [effect] etc.' *Boston Medical and Surgical Journal*, 1882.

walk,' and Aschenbrandt* has recently reported how Bavarian soldiers, who were feeling really shattered after strenuous activities and debilitating illnesses, were in a condition, after coca had been administered to them, to take part in exercises and marches. Moréno y Maïz† was able to stay awake for whole nights by using coca. Mantegazza went for forty hours without nourishment under the influence of coca. We are therefore justified in assuming, that the effect of cocaine on Europeans is the same as that of coca leaves on the Indians of South America.

The effect of a moderate dose of cocaine wears off so gradually, that it is difficult in normal circumstances to determine its length. If one works intensively under the influence of cocaine, a reduction in the sense of well-being sets in after three to five hours, and one needs a further dose of coca to prevent oneself from feeling tired. If one does not undertake heavy muscular work, the effect of the coca seems to last longer. All reports are in complete agreement that the state of euphoria caused by coca is not followed by any condition of weariness or other form of depression. On the contrary I tend to believe that a part of the effect of coca taken in moderate doses (0.05–0.10 grams) can last for over twenty-four hours. At least I have observed myself to be in a condition on the day after taking coca, which differed favourably from my usual one, and I would explain the possibility of a lasting increase in strength, which has often been asserted, as being caused by an accumulation of such after-effects.

That cocaine causes no disturbance of the organism with moderate use over a long time, is probable from observations to be reported later. Von Anrep has treated animals for thirty

* 'Die physiologische Wirkung und Bedeutung des Cocain. muriat. auf den menschlichen Organismus. Beobachtungen während der Herbstübungen des Jahres 1883 beim III baierischen Armee-Corps [beim II Bayer. A.C. 4. Div. 9. Reg. 2. Bat].'
† Loc. cit.

days with moderate doses of cocaine, without noticing any such harmful influences on bodily functions. It seems to me worth noting what I myself and other observers competent to judge have experienced, that after the first or repeated intake of coca absolutely no desire to use coca any more occurs, but there is rather a certain unmotivated aversion to the substance. Perhaps this circumstance has contributed to the fact that coca has not, despite a few enthusiastic recommendations, established itself as a stimulant in Europe.

The effect of large doses of coca was tested by Mantegazza on his own person. In doing so he got into a state of enormously heightened and happy awareness of life with a tendency to complete immobility, which was interrupted at times by the most intense urge to move around. The analogy with the results of the experiments on animals by von Anrep is thus unmistakable. With a further increase in the dose he continued, with an excessive pulse rate and a moderate raising of body temperature, to be in what he called a 'sopore beato'[2], and found his speech disturbed, his writing unsteady, and he finally had the most splendid and varied hallucinations, which were for a short time of a frightening nature but then became consistently brighter in mood. This drugged state caused by cocaine also left no depression and none of the symptoms of an intoxication which has been overcome. Moréno y Maïz has likewise observed a strong impulse to move around after larger doses of coca. No disturbance of consciousness occurred with Mantegazza even after taking eighteen drachmas of coca leaves; a pharmacist, who had taken 1.5 grams of cocaine, in order to poison himself,* became ill with symptoms of gastroenteritis without any dimming of consciousness.

* Ploss, *Zeitschrift für Chirurgie*, 1863.

VI. The Therapeutic Application of Coca

It could not fail to be the case that a plant, the consumption of which manifested such effects which were contemplated with amazement, would be applied, in that area where it was native, against the most varied disorders and organic illnesses. In a similarly uninhibited way coca was recommended by the first Europeans, who had become aware of this treasure of the indigenous population. Mantegazza later proposed, on the basis of his broad medical experience, a series of therapeutic indicators for coca, and first one and then the others found approval with other doctors. In the following I have endeavoured to bring together the recommendations concerning coca in the available literature and to distinguish those which are based on successes with patients from those which have been derived from consideration of the physiological effect of coca. In general the latter predominate. In North America there seems to be the prospect at present of the extensive use and recognition of coca preparations, while in Europe their names are hardly known to the majority of doctors. The unfavourable results, which were reported soon after the introduction of coca into Europe, the dubious quality, the scarcity and high price of the preparations explain this neglect of coca in Europe, which I am convinced is undeserved. Of those indicators which can be proposed for the use of cocaine, several have been unquestionably confirmed, and the others deserve at least unbiased testing. The cocaine and its salts produced by Merck are, as has been demonstrated, preparations which are imbued with the full or at least the essential effect of coca leaves.

a) Coca as Stimulant

The principal use of coca will probably remain that which the Indians have made of it for centuries: in every situation in which it is important to raise the physical capability of the body for a specified short time and to maintain it for new demands, especially when external circumstances prevent the rest and intake of nourishment appropriate to the harder work. Such as in war, on journeys, while climbing mountains, on expeditions, and such like, during which alcoholic drinks are also generally recognised to be valuable. Coca is a much more powerful and less harmful stimulant than alcohol, and only its high price stands in the way at present of it being used on a large scale. Based on the effect of coca on the indigenous people of South America, the old medical author Pedro Crespo (Lima, 1793) already recommended the introduction of coca into the European navy, as Neudörfer (1870), Clemens (1867) and Surgeon-Major E. Charles* did for the European armies, and Aschenbrandt's experiences could not have failed to attract the attention of the army leaders to coca. When giving cocaine as a stimulus it is best to repeat small effective doses (0.05–0.10 grams) often enough to ensure that the effect of one is combined with the effect of the next. An accumulation of cocaine does not seem to occur in the body; the complete absence of depressive states following the effect of coca has already been stressed.

How much one can expect coca to raise intellectual capability, cannot be judged at the moment with any certainty. My impression has been that the use of cocaine over a long time can bring about lasting improvement in cases in which inhibition has only physical causes and fatigue. The temporary effect of a dose of coca can certainly not be compared with that of an injection of morphine, but on the other hand one need not fear the general organic damage caused by chronic use of morphine.

To many doctors cocaine seemed destined to fill a gap in the medicinal resources of psychiatry, already known to have

* *Philadelphia Medical and Surgical Reporter*, 1883 [1882].

sufficient methods at its disposal to reduce the heightened excitement of nerve centres, but being aware of none, which would raise them from a state of reduced activity. Accordingly coca has been recommended for the most various kinds of weak psychic conditions: for hysteria, hypochondria, melancholic inhibition, stupor, and the like. Some successes have also been reported: the Jesuit Antonio Julian (Lima, 1787) reports that a learned missionary was freed from his extreme hypochondria by coca; Mantegazza praises coca for being almost always effective in those cases of functional disturbances, which we now include under the name of neurasthenia. For Fliessburg coca provided excellent help in cases of 'nervous prostration', and according to Caldwell* it is the best tonic for hysteria.

E. Morselli and G. Buccola[†] have conducted experiments on sufferers of melancholia with the systematic administration of cocaine over several months. They gave cocaine produced by Trommsdorf through subcutaneous injection in doses of 0.0025–0.10 grams. After 1–2 months they could confirm some slight improvement in their patients, who became more cheerful, took some nourishment and whose digestive tracts functioned more regularly.[‡]

On the whole the indications are that the effects of coca on nervous and weak psychic conditions requires further investigation, which will probably lead to a result which is favourable to some extent. For organic changes and conditions of inflammation of the nervous system coca is useless according to Mantegazza, and sometimes dangerous.

---

* 'Review of some of our later remedies.' *Detroit Th. G.* [*Detroit Therapeutic Gazette*] December 1880.
† 'Ricerche sperimentali sull'azione fisiologica e terapeutica della Cocaina.' *Rendiconti del R. 1st. Lombardo XIV*, 1882 [1881].
‡ Their reports on the physiological effects of cocaine agree with those of Mantegazza. They observed the immediate effects of cocaine injections to be: dilation of the pupils, an increase in temperature of up to 1.2°, a quickening of the pulse and of respiration. Nothing bad ever happens.

b) Coca in Cases of Disturbances in the Digestive Process of the Stomach

This is the oldest and best justified application of coca, and at the same time the one we are closest to understanding. According to the information, on which the oldest as well as the most recent authors (Julian, Martius, Unanué, Mantegazza, Bingel,[*] Scrivener,[†] Frankl, and others) all agree, coca, in all its different preparations, eliminates dyspeptic problems, and the bad mood and weakness which result from them, and brings about a lasting cure when used over a long time. I have personally been able to make a series of such observations.

Just as Mantegazza[‡] and Frankl[§] experienced it in themselves, I have also observed that embarrassing problems which occur after heavy meals, such as a feeling of pressure and fullness in the stomach, discomfort and a disinclination to work, wear off with some belching after small doses of cocaine (0.025–0.05 grams). I have provided some colleagues repeatedly with the same kind of relief and twice been able to observe, how nausea following gastric excesses succumbed after a short time to the effect of cocaine and gave way to a normal desire to eat and a subjective feeling of well-being. I have also learned to avoid stomach problems by ingesting sodium salicylate, with the addition of a small amount of cocaine.

My respected colleague, Dr Josef Pollak, has provided me with the following observation of a striking effect of cocaine, which shows, that not only the unpleasant subjective sensations relating to the stomach can be neutralised by cocaine, but also

* *Pharmakologisch-therapeutisches Handbuch*, Erlangen, 1862.
† Loc. cit. 'an excellent tonic in weakness of the stomach'.
‡ Mantegazza's detailed case histories convince me thoroughly of their credibility.
§ 'Report on coca by Dr Josef Frankl, spa doctor in Marienbad.' *Zeitschrift der K. Gesellschaft der Ärzte* [*Zeitschrift der kaiserlichen-königlichen Gesellschaft der Ärtze*] 1860.

strong reflex phenomena, so that one must attribute far-reaching effects on the mucous membrane and the musculature of this organ to cocaine.

A robust forty-two-year-old man, well known to the doctor, has been forced to keep strictly to a certain diet and to specific mealtimes, otherwise he will never be able to avoid the occurrence of the incidents to be described. When he is travelling and also when influenced by his emotions he proves to be especially sensitive. The attacks occur very regularly, beginning in the evening with a feeling of discomfort in the epigastrium; then a strong pain in the forehead occurs with reddening of the face, tears in the eyes, and a throbbing of the carotid arteries, together with the deepest depression and apathy; the night is spent in a sleepless condition, and towards morning there is long-lasting and painful vomiting; towards midday he becomes calmer, but while consuming a few spoonfuls of soup there is a feeling 'as if a heavy ball, which had been lying inside him for a long time, was finally being heaved away'. Then there is some rancid belching, until he returns to his normal condition towards evening. The whole day the patient is incapable of work and must stay in bed.

On 10 June at 8 o'clock in the evening the usual precursors of an attack appeared; at 10 o'clock, when the heavy headache had developed, the patient received 0.075 grams of cocaine muriaticum. Soon after this there was a feeling of warm belching, which seemed to the patient to be 'still not much'. At 10.30 he was given another dose of 0.075 grams of cocaine: the belching becomes stronger; the patient feels lighter in mood, and is able to write quite a long letter. He asserts that he feels strong movements in his stomach, and at 12 o'clock, apart from a light headache, feels normal and even cheerful. He goes for an hour's walk, cannot sleep till 3 o'clock in the morning, which does not seem annoying to him, and then wakes up the next morning feeling healthy, strong enough to work, and with a good appetite.

The effect of cocaine on the stomach is, as Mantegazza also assumes, a twofold one: the stimulation of movements and the reduction of the sensitivity of the stomach. The latter is likely not only because of the subjective sensations after consuming cocaine but also because of the analogous effect of the cocaine on other mucous membranes. Mantegazza claims to have achieved the most excellent results with gastralgias and intestinal pains, and with all painful and spasmodic affections of the stomach and the intestines, which he explains by the anaesthetising quality of coca. In this respect I cannot confirm Mantegazza's experiences; I observed only once during the course of a case of gastroenteritis how the sensitivity of the stomach to pressure diminished after taking coca; on other occasions I myself saw and heard also from other doctors, that patients, in whom an ulcer or a scar in the stomach was suspected, complained about an increase in pains after using coca. This fact can be explained by the increase in stomach movements.

As definite grounds for using coca I should therefore like to cite atonic weakness in digestion and the so-called nervous stomach disorders. With these conditions it should be possible to achieve not only relief from symptoms but also lasting improvement.

c) Coca in the Case of Cachexia

The extensive use of coca is also urgently to be recommended and has also allegedly been tried successfully in all those pathological states which are accompanied by tissue consumption:

serious cases of anaemia, phthisis, long-lasting illnesses with fever and such like, and finally during convalescence from such conditions. Thus McBean* observed a constant rate of improvement when using coca in the case of typhoid fever, and with phthisis it is shown to have an influence in reducing the fever and in lessening perspiration. Peckham[†] reports a case definitely identified as phthisis, in which there was conspicuous improvement after the use of a fluid extract of coca over a seven-month period, and Hole* reports another, rather dubious case, in which a chronic loss of appetite had led to extreme wasting away and exhaustion. R. Bartholow[†] has observed generally in the case of phthisis and other 'draining processes' the favourable effect of coca; Mantegazza and several other authors ascribe the same effect to coca, which is of inestimable value for therapy, of reducing physical decline in cases of cachexia and of increasing strength.

It is possible to try and trace these successes partly to the unquestionably favourable effect of coca on the digestive process in the stomach, but one must keep it in mind, that a large number of the writers on coca regard it as an 'economic measure', that is to say that they are of the opinion, that an organism, which has consumed an extremely small amount of cocaine, is able to obtain a larger amount of living energy[3] from the same dissolved elements, which can be transmuted into work, than it can without coca.[‡] With a rate of work which remains constant an organism which has been given cocaine should be able to survive with little absorption of material, and thus with little consumption of nourishment.

---

* 'Erythroxylon Coca in the treatment of typhus and typhoid fevers, and also of other febrile diseases.' *British Medical Journal*, Vol I for 1877.
† *Detroit Therapeutic Gazette*, July 1880.
* 'Coca Erythroxylon in exhaustion.' *Detroit Th. G.* [*Detroit Therapeutic Gazette*], Oct 1880.
† *Detroit Th. G.* [*Detroit Therapeutic Gazette*], Sept [May] 1880, according to the *Louisville Medical News*.
‡ Marvaud, *Les aliments d'épargne*, Paris 1874.

This assumption was evidently made in explanation of what von Voit[*] claimed to be the failure to understand the effect of cocaine on the Indians. It also does not necessarily involve a contradiction of the law of the conservation of energy. For in accomplishing work at the cost of nourishment or tissue components a certain loss occurs, either in making use of the dissolved materials or in conversion of the energy gained during work. This loss can perhaps be reduced by making suitable arrangements. But such a process has not been proven. Experiments on the amount of urine emissions with and without the use of coca have not provided results which concur with each other, and have probably not always been conducted in conditions, in which they could in themselves be conclusive. What is more, these experiments seem to have been made with the premiss that one could discover in urine emission, which is known not to be changed through work, a measure of the general absorption of material. Thus Christison observed a slight reduction in the solids contained in urine during the walks taken with the aid of coca. Lippmann, Demarle, Marvaud and recently Mason[†] likewise draw the conclusion from their experiments, that the consumption of coca reduces the amount of urine emitted, but Gazeau[‡] on the other hand has confirmed an increase of 11–24% in urine emission under the effect of coca and explains the ability to do without nourishment and the capacity for work when using coca by the better disposal of the substances accumulated in the body. The emission of carbonic acid has not been made the subject of any investigations.

Von Voit has demonstrated that coffee, which was also considered to be an 'economic measure', has no influence on the

[*] 'Physiologie des allgem. Stoffwechsels', 1881. *Hermanns Handbuch* [der Physiologie] VI. 1.
[†] 'Erythroxylon coca, its physiological effect and especially its effect on the excretion of urea by the kidneys.' *Boston Med. and Surg. Journal* [Boston Medical and Surgical Journal], 1882.
[‡] *Comptes rendus de l'Académie des sciences*, II, 1870.

decomposition of protein. One must consider the conception of coca as an 'economic measure' to have been undermined by experiments in which animals were allowed to suffer hunger with and without cocaine, and the reduction in bodily weight as well as how long they could avoid inanition was determined. Such experiments have been conducted by Claude Bernard,[*] Moréno y Maïz, Demarle, Gazeau and von Anrep, and the results show that animals given cocaine succumb to inanition just as quickly, and perhaps a little more quickly, than those not given it. In apparent contradiction of this is the report by Unanué of an experiment provided by history concerning the starvation of the city of La Paz, in which those inhabitants who had consumed coca escaped death by starvation. In this context one can cite the fact that in humans the nervous system has an unquestionable, albeit mysterious, influence on the nourishing of tissue. After all, a healthy human being can become thinner under the influence of the psyche. The therapeutic grounds with which we started cannot therefore be dismissed straight away; the excitement of the nervous centres by cocaine can have a favourable influence on nourishing the body in cases of consumption, even if this does not consist of a slowing down of the metabolic rate.

One should add here, that coca has also received enthusiastic praise for its effects in cases of syphilis. R.W. Taylor[†] asserts that more mercury can be tolerated and mercury cachexia held at bay through the simultaneous use of coca, and J. Collan[‡] recommends it as the best remedy for stomatitis mercurialis and reports that Pagvalin always prescribes it together with mercury preparations.

[*] In Marvaud [1874].
[†] 'Pathology and Treatment in venereal diseases' in *Detroit Th. G.* [*Detroit Therapeutic Gazette*], February, 1884.
[‡] Loc. cit.

d) Coca in the Curing of Morphine and Alcohol Addiction

In recent years the most important observation has been made in America, that coca preparations possess the power of suppressing the craving for morphine among habitual morphine addicts and of reducing to a low level the symptoms of severe collapse which occur in curing morphine addiction. According to the information which I have drawn mostly from the *Detroit Therapeutic Gazette*, it was W.H. Bentley who announced in May 1878 that he had replaced the usual alkaloid used by a woman addicted to morphine with coca. It seems that Palmer aroused widespread interest in this method of treating morphine addiction two years later through an essay in the *Louisville Medical News*, for the heading 'Erythroxylon coca in the opium habit' becomes a standard one over the next two years for the reports of the *Therapeutic Gazette*. From then on the reports of successful courses of withdrawal treatment become rarer. Whether this was a result of the treatment becoming established or of it being given up, I have no knowledge. From the announcements by traders in the recent numbers of American newspapers I would tend to think the former were the case.

There are about sixteen communications which report successful withdrawals, and only on one occasion is there a report that coca had let a morphine addict down, and to which the doctor had added a query about what the reason was for all the enthusiastic recommendations to use coca for morphine addiction.* The successful cases vary greatly in their value as evidence: in some it involves very large doses of opium or morphine and addiction over many years. There are few reports about recidivists, as cases are mostly reported very soon after the cure. The symptoms during abstinence are not always reported in detail; of special value are those reports, to which the comment is added, that the patients gave up the coca preparation after a few weeks,

* [Snipes] D.T.G. [*Detroit Therapeutic Gazette*] Nov, 1880.

without feeling any recurrence of the desire for morphine.* It is stressed many times that morphine cachexia gave way to a condition of the most radiant health, so that the patients were hardly recognisable.† Concerning the actual method used during withdrawal, it must be stated that in the majority of cases a gradual reduction of the habitual dose accompanied by a rising increase in the coca dosage was preferred. But some abrupt withdrawals were undertaken.‡ For the latter cases Palmer prescribes repeating a specific dose of coca as many times a day as the craving for morphine recurs.§ The daily amount of cocaine used is gradually reduced in the process, until the antidote can be completely dispensed with. From the start there were few accidents during the period of abstinence or they became less severe after a few days. Almost all withdrawal treatments were carried out by the patients themselves, while the necessary prerequisite of curing morphine addiction without the aid of coca, as it is conducted in Europe, is supervision of the patient in a sanatorium.

I had the opportunity of observing the abrupt withdrawal from morphine by using coca in a man, who had suffered greatly from the most severe symptoms of abstinence during earlier withdrawal treatment.[4] His condition was bearable on this occasion, and there was no depression or nausea as long as the effect of the coca lasted. The only permanent symptoms which made one aware of his abstinence were a feeling of coldness and diarrhoea. The patient did not have to stay in bed, was

* J. Brenton [Benton], *T.G.* [*Detroit Therapeutic Gazette*] March 1881 – G.H. Gray from 'The Medical Brief', *T.G.* [*Detroit Therapeutic Gazette*] June 1881 – H. Leforger, Dec. 1872 [G. Leforger, Nov. 1882].

† E.C. Huse, *T.G.* [*Detroit Therapeutic Gazette*] Sept 1880 – Henderson, *T.G.* [*Detroit Therapeutic Gazette*] February 1881.

‡ R. Taggart, *T.G.* [*Detroit Therapeutic Gazette*] May 1881 – A.F. Stimmel, *T.G.* [*Detroit Therapeutic Gazette*][April and] June, 1881.

§ *T.G.* [*Detroit Therapeutic Gazette*] July 1880. The preparation employed was mostly the fluid extract produced by Parke, Davis and Co.

able to work and consumed 3 decigrams of *cocainum muriaticum* at a time during the first few days. After ten days he was able to give up the cure.

In curing morphine addiction it is not a question of some kind of exchange, by which a morphine addict becomes a *coquero*, but of the temporary use of coca. I also do not believe that it is the generally strengthening effect of the coca, which enables the organism weakened by morphine to get over the withdrawal from morphine with only minor symptoms. I tend rather to assume that a directly antagonistic effect against the morphine must be attributed to the coca, and in support of this opinion I can report a case, which I borrow from the observations of Dr Josef Pollak:

> A thirty-three-year-old woman has been suffering for years from severe menstrual migraine, which can only be allevi- ated by an injection of morphine. Although the woman never takes morphine nor experiences a craving for it during the periods when she is free of the migraine, she behaves like a morphine addict during her attacks. A few hours after the injection there occur extreme depression, attacks of nausea and vomiting, which are terminated by a further injection of morphine. Following this the symptoms of intolerance occur again, so that an attack of migraine together with its consequences confines the patient to her bed in a wretched state for three days. Cocaine was then employed against the migraine, but it proved to be useless. It was necessary to fall back on morphine injections, but when the symptoms of morphine intolerance occurred, they were quickly removed by 1 decigram of cocaine, so that the patient got over her attack in a much shorter time and used much less morphine.

At the same time as it was being used against morphine addiction, coca was also being used in America against chronic alcoholism and reported on in relation to this.* In this case also unquestionable successes were achieved, the irresistible desire to drink was overcome or alleviated, and the dyspeptic problems of the drinker were improved. The suppression of the craving for alcohol through coca proved to be generally more difficult than that of morphine addiction. Bentley reports that in one case a drinker became a *coquero*. What huge significance for the national economy coca might acquire as an 'economic measure', in another sense of the term, if its effectiveness in curing drinkers of their addiction were confirmed, one need only hint at.

e) The Use of Coca against Asthma

Tschudi and Markham[†] report that, through chewing coca leaves, they were protected while climbing the Andes against the so-called mountain sickness, a complex of symptoms consisting of dyspnoea, a pounding heart, dizziness and so on. Poizat[‡] reports that a patient's asthmatic attacks can always be checked by use of coca. I cite this characteristic of coca, because it seems to permit a physiological explanation. Premature paralysis of some of the branches of the cranial nerves occurred in the animal experiments of von Anrep, and altitude sickness, as well as the attacks in chronic bronchitis, can be interpreted as reflex reactions of the lung branches of the cranial nerve. The application of coca should be considered in cases of other kinds of cranial nerve disorders.[5]

---

* W.H. Bentley [W.D. Bentley], *T.G.* [*Detroit Therapeutic Gazette*] Sept. 80 – Volum [Vollum] Jan, 1881 – H. Warner, March, 81. – Stimmel, April and July 81.

† *Travels in Peru and India*, 1862.

‡ 'The Erythroxylon coca in Asthma.' *Philadelphia Medical and Surgical Reporter*, 1881.

f) Coca as an Aphrodisiac

The indigenous people of South America, who represented their Goddess of Love with coca leaves in her hand, had no doubt about the effect of coca in exciting the genital region. Mantegazza confirms that the *coqueros* retain a high level of potency into old age, and also reports cases of the restoration of potency and the decline in manifestations of functional weakness after using cocaine, but tends to believe that this effect of coca does not occur in all individuals. Marvaud defends categorically the stimulating effect of coca, other authors recommend coca very strongly for functional weakness and temporary exhaustion, and Bentley reports a case which belongs in this context.*

Among the people to whom I gave coca, three of them have reported intense sexual excitement to me, which they related without second thoughts to the coca. A young writer, who after being in a bad mood for a long time was enabled by coca to start work, refrained from using coca because of these side effects which he found unwelcome.

g) Local Application of Coca

The characteristic of cocaine and its salts to anaesthetise the skin and the mucous membrane, when it comes into contact with them in concentrated solution, encourages its occasional use especially in affections of the mucous membrane. According to Collin,† Ch. Fauvel praises the use of cocaine in the treatment of pharynx infections and describes it as 'le tenseur par excellence des chordes vocales'.[6] Cocaine must prove to have several applications based on its anaesthetising property.

* *T.G.* [*Detroit Therapeutic Gazette*] Dec. [Sept.], 1880 [Bentley's article does *not* actually refer to coca as an aphrodisiac].
† 'De la coca et de ses [et ses] véritables propriétés thérapeutiques.' *L'Union médicale*, 1877.

Letter to Martha: 16 January, 1885

Vienna, Friday, 16 January, 1885

My sweet darling,

Warm heartfelt greetings to you for the seventeenth. Do you know, incidentally, that it was on a seventeenth that my course started? And now quickly to my news, so that you can feel glad straightaway. The die is cast. Today I've had my unruly beard cut and went to Nothnagel, to whom I sent in my card, with the inscription '… takes the liberty of asking, if and when the Herr Hofrat would be willing to grant him audience on an important personal matter.' There was the usual pushing and shoving, and the usual anxious whispering of the people around me, about whether I was also a doctor and should thus be allowed in before them, who had been waiting so long. I could understand most clearly a conversation between a lady in mourning and her brother. Her female perspicacity immediately diagnosed something dubious about me, while the brother rejected with a superior smile the suspicion that I might belong to that class of people who would do them any harm. Finally they were disappointed, because I was in there ahead of them all facing the man, who had so often played a decisive role for me, with that picture behind him again of his sensible, serious dead wife. I asked briefly, whether I should present my request now, or later. He was of the opinion, that if it was brief, I should present it now, otherwise it would be better for us to confer on the matter at another time. I promised to be brief.

'You once expressed the wish to be of help to me, and because you said this, I believe that you meant it. There is now an opportunity to do so. I wish to inquire of you whether, on the basis of my works so far, I should now seek a lectureship, or whether I should wait till I have produced more.'

'What are all the works you have produced, my dear Doctor. There's the one on coca…' (So coca is the first thing associated with my name).

I interrupted him, drawing out the pack of my collected writings, both those from the period before Martha and those of the later one. He just counted the number.

'It's eight or nine in number,' he said, 'Oh God, you can confidently make a submission. What kind of person do you have to be for them to deny you a lectureship? There won't be any trouble in the least.'

'But I have got several things to publish, two of them in the very near future.'

'You don't need them. That's more than enough.'

'And at the moment there's not much on nervous pathology among them.'

'That's not important. Who can understand nervous pathology, without having tackled anatomy and physiology? Three will be chosen to provide references, Meynert, Bamberger and me probably. No protest will be raised, and if any reservations are expressed in the institute, then we're man enough to support our case, aren't we?'

'So may I assume that you support my application for a lectureship? I know that Meynert will without more ado.'

'Certainly, and I don't think that anyone will object to it, but if they do, then we'll manage to push it through anyway.'

I added: 'There's the matter of confirming the status of some courses which I am giving unofficially. It's true I'm giving them only to English students in the English language, but they come in droves.'

Then we shook hands firmly, and I went away as the newest lecturer. I'll make my submission next week. You won't fail to get your golden serpent this time.

With one heartfelt kiss which must stand for many,

Your Sigmund

'A Contribution to Knowledge about the Effect of Coca', January 1885

In the July issue of the *Zentralblatt für Therapie* I published a study on the coca plant and its alkaloid cocaine,* which deserved the attention of doctors because of its examination of the experiences included in the literature and of my own. I may say that the success of my proposals was unexpectedly rapid and complete. While Dr L. Königstein undertook at my own request to test the effectiveness of cocaine as an analgesic and in reducing secretion in pathological conditions of the eye, my colleague in this hospital, Dr Karl Koller, had the good idea, independently of my own suggestion, of bringing about complete anaesthesia of the cornea and the conjunctiva by the use of cocaine, the numbing influence of which on the sensitivity of the mucous membrane has been long known,† and he has further proven the high practical value of local anaesthesia through experiments on animals and operations on human beings. As a result of Koller's report on this matter to this year's congress of eye-specialists in Heidelberg, cocaine has gained general acceptance as a local anaesthetic.

As a continuation of my studies on cocaine I have attempted to formulate the marvellous general effect of this alkaloid, which consists in a heightening of one's mood, of physical and intellectual capability and of stamina, by means of objective indicators and by taking measurements of it. I felt driven to this undertaking by the experience of the fact that the subjective symptoms of the effect of cocaine manifest themselves differently in different people. While many report a state of

* 'Über Coca,' *Centralblatt f. d. ges.Therapie*. [*Centralblatt für die gesamte Therapie*] II Jahrgang, VII, Juli, 1884.
† The seventh of the indicators which I proposed for the use of cocaine concerns local application and finishes with the words, 'Cocaine must prove to have several applications based on its anaesthetising property.'

euphoria, which is much more splendid than that which I have described as having myself, others feel uncomfortable after cocaine, confused, and under some distinctly poisonous influence. Schroff, the elder, who was the first (1862) to be able to test the effect of cocaine, seems to have belonged to the latter group. And this chance personal disposition is partly to blame for the longstanding neglect which has affected the alkaloid. From an objective method of testing it I would thus also expect that it would reveal greater uniformity in the effect of coca.

As a means of characterising the effect of cocaine by the identification of measurable quantities, perhaps of various kinds, I chose to test the motor strength of a particular group of muscles and the time taken for mental reactions. The first test was carried out using a dynamometer, a springy metal clasp, which when pressed together pushes a pointer along a graduated scale, in such a way that it stops after the pressure is released. I had two such instruments at my disposal, a heavier one, which provided more conspicuous results, because one could press it with both hands, but had the disadvantage that it required a large expenditure of energy and made one tired quickly, and a lighter dynamometer as constructed by Dr Von Burq to be pressed with one hand. I soon began to trust the information provided by the dynamometer, because I found that the effects of the pressure, especially its maximum values, are to a large extent independent of the arbitrary action of the person pressing, and the way the pressure is applied allows only few and insignificant variations. The testing of mental reaction times was done with the Exner *Neuramöbimeter*, which consists essentially of a metal spring, which is tuned at one hundred oscillations per second, and the vibration of which is interrupted by the subject, as soon as he notices the sound caused by relaxing the fixed spring. The time which lasts from hearing the sound till lifting the spring, is the reaction time and is given directly in hundredths of seconds by the number of oscillations recorded by the spring. Concerning the precise setting up of this small piece of equipment and the precautions necessary with such experiments I refer the reader to 'The Experimental Examination of the Simplest Mental Processes'. Dr Herzig was kind enough to undertake these somewhat laborious experiments with me.

I have conducted both sequences of tests repeatedly on myself, or rather had someone conduct them on me. I know that such experiments on oneself have the unfortunate consequence for the person who conducts them of demanding two kinds of credibility relating to the same matter, but I had to do it for extraneous reasons and because none of the individuals who were available for me to use exhibited such a uniform reaction to cocaine. The results of my investigation were however confirmed through my testing of other persons, mainly colleagues.

The result of the dynamometer test was that 0.05–0.10 grams of *cocaine muriaticum significantly increases the motor strength*, and what is more the maximum effect occurs in me after ten to fifteen minutes at the same time as the coca euphoria and it persists at a somewhat lower level for several hours. I include a report of some experiments in greater detail:

Experiment I, on 9 November, 1884. Using the two-handed dynamometer, Pressure given in pounds. To study the effect of tiredness, pressure was applied three times in quick succession at each attempt.

Times	Pressure values	Maximum values	Medium values	Remarks
8 am	66–65–60	66	63.6	On an empty stomach
10.00	67–55–50	67	57.3	After doctor's round
10.22	67–63–56	67	62	After breakfast
10.30	65–58–67	67	63.6	
10.33	0.10 g cocaine muriaticum			
10.45	82–75–69	82	75.3	Followed by first belching
10.55	76–69–64	76	69.6	Tired
11.20	78–71–77	78	75.3	Euphoria
12.30	72–66–74	74	70.6	Before lunch
12.55	77–73–67	77	72.6	–
13.35	75–66–74	75	71.6	After lunch
13.50	76–71–61	76	69.3	–
15.35	65–58–62	65	61.6	Euphoria over

As can be seen, the cocaine has caused a considerable increase in motor strength, lasting about five hours, whether this is judged by the maximum or the medium figures in the table above. My general condition on the day of the experiment was bad and my motor strength low.

Another experiment shows the effect of coca with higher initial figures for motor strength.

Experiment II, on 10 November, 1884. The same dynamometer.

Times	Pressure values	Maximum values	Medium values	Remarks
8 am	60	60	60	Tired
10.00	72–63–67	73	67.6	After doctor's round
– Followed by a small unspecified amount of cocaine				
10.20	76–70–76	76	74	Cheerful
10.30	73–70–68	73	70.3	–
11.35	72–72–74	74	72.6	–
12.50	74–73–63	74	70	–
14.20	70–68–69	70	69	–
16.00	76–74–75	76	75	Normal condition
18.00	67–64–58	67	63	After concentrated work
20.30	74–64–67	74	68.3	Somewhat tired
– Followed by 0.1 g cocaine muriaticum				
20.43	80–73–74	80	75.6	Belching
20.58	79–76–71	79	75.3	–
21.18	77–72–67	77	72	Feeling of lightness

After continuing such experiments over several weeks, two facts were quite noticeable: firstly, *that the figures for the motor strength of one group of muscles during one day reveal a regular pattern of variation, and secondly, that these attain completely different absolute values on different days.* These are matters which have no relation to the effect of coca itself, but are perhaps sufficiently interesting to merit a few remarks.

The following table provides evidence of the course of daily variation in motor strength in me:

Experiments on 27 and 28 November, 1884. Pressure in kilograms. Burq's dynamometer. The figures correspond to maximum values after pressing with the right hand three times.

November 27			November 28		
Times	Maximal values	Remarks	Times	Maximal values	Remarks
7.00	32	On getting up	7.20	32	On getting up
9.30	35	After doctor's round, normal	7.50	34–5	On an empty stomach
12.00	37+	After working for several hours	10.00	37	After doctor's round
14.45	37-	After coffee, otherwise nothing	10.30	36–7	After breakfast
16.00	38	After a lecture	13.40	36	After work
17.45	37+	After three hours' work	14.40	36	After lecture
18.45	38-	–	16.00	36	After lecture
19.15	35+	Tired	17.30	36	After doctor's rounds
20.00	36.5	Resting	20.30	37	After coffee
21.15	34	After supper	22.20	35+	After supper

From these as from all other observations it emerges, that motor strength is at its lowest in the morning – it has not completely woken up, as it were – and that it then quickly increases, to reach a high level during the forenoon period, at which it stays throughout the day, and then slowly but constantly declines in the evening, but not as far as the morning minimum. As long as it did not lead to heavy tiredness, concentrated work seemed to me more likely to raise the motor capacity. I could not identify any influence of taking meals or of leaving them out. The thought naturally suggests itself, that the diurnal variation in motor strength might be related to the daily temperature graph.

After I had completed these observations I became aware of a provisional report by Dr Max Buch,* which deals with the diurnal variations in motor strength. Buch's information differs from mine only in so far as he finds a decline after a maximum value in the afternoon to a second, lower maximum value in the evening, which is then followed by the nightly fall. Whether the differences in our way of life, or the fact that Buch conducted his investigations with an instrument graduated in smaller units (¼ kg), was responsible for the small difference in our results, remains to be seen. Buch mentions also an inaugural dissertation by Powarnin,† in which the essential fact of the minimal level of strength in the morning is already stressed.

I have also cited the second remarkable fact, that motor strength attains different values on different days, so that their diurnal variation ranges over a higher and a lower level. Thus I have recorded many days, on which I began with a minimum of 28 kg and could obtain no higher maximum value than 35 kg. The highest difference between the daily maximum and the minimum amounted to 6 kg in my case, but the highest difference between corresponding figures on different days on the other hand was only 4 kg.

It seems to me undoubtedly true that the latter variation in motor strength, which is dependent on the time of day, is an expression of one's general condition, the subjective manifestation of which, as general feeling and mood, contains an element relating to motor capability. I would rather not consider the effect of coca itself to be a direct one – on, for example, the motor elements in nerves or on muscles – but as an indirect one,

* 'Über die Tagesschwankungen der Muskelkraft des Menschen.' *Berliner Klin. Wochenschr.* [*Berliner Klinische Wochenschrift*] Number 28, 1884.
† 'On the Influence of Sleep on Human Muscle Strength.' [Russian] Petersburg 1883.

brought about by creating a better general condition. Two factors support this view: firstly, the fact that the most notable increase in motor strength occurs so quickly after the consumption of cocaine, at a time when admittedly the euphoria caused by the cocaine has developed, but when all of the cocaine can hardly have been absorbed into the blood stream; and secondly, the fact that the increase in motor strength is more considerable when cocaine exerts its effect at a time of poor bodily condition and reduced motor energy. The figures attained under the influence of cocaine at such times still exceed the maximum values in normal circumstances.

If one takes into account the values of physical constants ascertainable on living beings in characterising the condition of an individual, then naturally those figures will deserve priority, which, like temperature, show no considerable individual variations. To characterise the various conditions of a specific individual person one should not leave out of consideration the motor strength of a particular group of muscles.

The experiments on the influence of cocaine on reaction times have provided a similar and generally less clear result. I noticed several times that my reaction times under the influence of cocaine were shorter and more uniform than before consuming coca, but I had just as favourable conditions for my mental reactions, if I was in a cheerful and productive mood. The change in the reaction time is due therefore to the euphoria produced by coca, to which I have also attributed the increase in muscle strength.

Experiment I, on 26 November, 1884:

Times	Reaction Times	Maximum Values	Minimum Values	Average	Remarks
19.10	15½ –21½–19– 21–18½– 24–24	24	15½	For 7 attempts 20.5	Motor strength, 36, tired

At 19.30 cocaine muriaticum 0.10 g

Times	Reaction Times	Maximum Values	Minimum Values	Average	Remarks
19.38	17–21½– 16–21– 17–16	2½	16	for 6 attempts 18	motor strength 39+
20.05	17–17– 18–17	18	17	for 4 attempts 17.2	A little more cocaine
20.15	3½–11– 16–15– 16–12	16	11	for 6 attempts 13.9	Euphoria
20.30	15½– 14½–15– 13½– 17½	17½	14½	for 5 attempts 15.2	Continuous well-being, motor energy, 37.5

Experiment II, on 4 December, 1884, in excellent condition without cocaine:

Times	Reaction Times	Maximum Values	Minimum Values	Average	Remarks
20.15	13½–13–14½–13½	14½	13	For 4 attempts 13.6	Motor energy 38–39 kilos
20.30	15–14–14–19 – 15½–15½	19	14	for 6 attempts 15.5	Disturbing noise during 4th reaction
20.45	11½–13½–14½–12½–16½	16½	12½	for 5 attempts 13.7	–
21.00	12½–13–13–15½–14–18½	18½	12½	for 6 attempts 14.2	Motor energy 38

Addenda, February, 1885

1. On the Effect of Coca on Healthy People

Since publication of the treatise reprinted above, I had the opportunity of observing the effect of cocaine on a larger number of people, and after the experiences obtained thereby I must emphasise even more strongly the variety of individual reactions to cocaine. I have discovered both individuals who displayed a coca-euphoria which corresponded completely with my own, also some who did not feel any influence from doses of 0.05–0.10 grams, and yet others who reacted to it with a light state of intoxication characterised by talkativeness and a dizzy condition. On the other hand the increase in capability seemed to me to be a constant symptom of the effect of coca, and, prompted by such experiences, I have undertaken an experiment to demonstrate the effect of coca through the changes in measurable amounts in living beings and to measure them while observing them. The results of this experiment have been published in the *Wiener medicinischen Wochenschrift* of 31 January, 1885, and refer to the testing of the muscle strength of the arm by means of a dynamometer and to the testing of mental reaction times with the aid of the instrument provided by Prof. Exner, the *Neuramöbimeter*. I was able to confirm on my own person that the pressing strength of one hand was increased through the intake of 0.10 grams of cocaine muriaticum by 2–4 kilos, and the pressing strength of both hands by 4–6 kilos. It is interesting to note at the same time, that the effect of the coca is dependent on the particular condition of the experimental subject, and is shown more clearly evident in the low initial numbers recorded for motor strength than in the high ones. The increase in motor strength caused by coca occurs suddenly after fifteen minutes and ceases after a gradual decline over 4–5 hours. This increase runs parallel to the euphoria caused by the coca and seems to derive rather from the prevailing readiness to work and the improvement in the general condition, than from a direct influence on the motor system. A change in the mental reaction time was also observed. The latter turned out in my case to be as it is when I am feeling at my best, if, before taking cocaine, it had been unsteady and lengthened, which corresponds to being in a worse condition. The increase in muscle strength caused by cocaine as demonstrated by the dynamometer can be considered conclusive authentication of the reports of the effect of coca on the Indians.

2. On the Coca Effect in Morphine Addiction

The applicability of cocaine in cases of morphine collapse has recently been confirmed by Richter (Pankow), 1885, and the same author has also supported the assertion in the present text of the antagonistic relationship between the effects of cocaine and morphine.

3. On the Internal Application of Cocaine

As at present several authors, in unjustified anxiety, seem to fear some bad effects from the internal application of cocaine, it seems not at all pointless to stress, that even subcutaneous injections, which I have successfully made in a case of long-lasting sciatica, are completely harmless.[7] The toxic dose is very high for humans, and there does not seem to be a lethal one.

4. On the Local Effect of Cocaine

This characteristic of the use of coca has received general recognition through its application by Koller in the anaesthetisation of the cornea, and through the works of Königstein, Jelinek and countless others, and ensures cocaine's lasting value among the wealth of medications available. It is to be expected that the internal application of cocaine will lead to equally pleasing results. However, the present price of the material which has been raised even higher, presents an obstacle to all further experiments.

'On the General Effect of Cocaine', March, 1885

A Lecture held at the Psychiatric Society on 5 March, 1885, by Dr Sigmund Freud

Last summer I engaged in a study of the physiological effect and therapeutic application of cocaine and have presented myself before you to give this lecture because I believe that some aspects of the topic could also arouse the interest of a psychiatric society. In so doing I leave aside completely the external application of cocaine, which has been introduced so successfully into the medical treatment of eyes and has also achieved very fruitful results in other branches of practical medicine. Our interest concerns only the effect of cocaine when applied internally.

Through the conquest of the countries of South America, it has become generally known, that the leaves of the coca plant are used by the natives there as a stimulant, and the effect of the consumption of coca is said, according to the most reliable people who have reported it, to consist in marvellous productive capability. It is understandable therefore that great hopes were cherished in Europe, when a quantity of coca leaves was brought to Europe by the Novara expedition, and Neumann, a student of Wöhler's in Göttingen, produced a new alkaloid, cocaine, from it. With this substance, as with the leaves themselves, many experiments have since been carried out, to obtain a result similar to the effect of coca on the Indians, but the general effect of these efforts was great disappointment and the tendency to doubt the credibility of those reports from the countries where coca was grown. I will not go into the probable reason for this failure here; in any case there do exist some reports from that time – about sixty or seventy years ago – which testify to an increase in productive capability caused by cocaine. In the winter of 1883 Dr von Aschenbrandt reported that Bavarian soldiers, who had become worn out, as the result of influences which exhausted them, such as strain, heat, etc., recovered, after they had been given quite a small amount of cocaine muriaticum. The credit I claim consists only perhaps in the fact that I believed in this report. It was this which was the cause of my studying the effect of coca on my own person and on others.

I can describe the effect of cocaine applied internally as follows: if one takes the basic effective dose (0.05–0.10 grams) in the best condition of well-being and does not undertake any special exertion after it, then one will feel hardly any conspicuous effect. It is different however, if one takes this dose of cocaine hydrochloride during a lowering of one's general condition caused by tiredness or hunger. Then one feels after a short time (10–15 minutes) that one has been raised to the highest level of mental and physical freshness. One is in a state of euphoria, which differs from that after the consumption of alcohol by the absence of any feeling of change in one's condition. As surprising as this effect of the introduction of cocaine is, the absence of such characteristics, which might differentiate between this state and the euphoria which is normal in a healthy condition, has contributed to its being underestimated. As soon as one has forgotten the contrast between the present condition and that before taking cocaine, it is difficult to believe that one is under the influence of some foreign substance, and yet one is profoundly changed for 4–5 hours. For as long as the effect of the coca lasts, it is possible to perform mental and physical work with greater stamina, and those needs, which otherwise make themselves felt in a demanding way, such as rest, nourishment and sleep, appear to be dispelled. In the first hours after taking cocaine it is even impossible to sleep. This effect of the alkaloid gradually subsides after the time specified and is not followed by any depression.

In my treatise 'On Coca' (*Centralblatt für die gesammte Therapie*, edited by Heitler, July, 1884; printed separately by

Moritz Perles, 1885) I have cited several examples of the over-coming of genuine tiredness and a feeling of hunger and such like, which I have observed mainly in colleagues, who took cocaine at my request. I have had many similar experiences since then, as in the case of a writer, who had been incapable to literary production for weeks beforehand and, after a dose of 0.1 grams of cocaine muriaticum, was able to work for fourteen hours without interruption. But I could not fail to notice that individual disposition plays a great role in the effectiveness of cocaine, perhaps a greater one than with other alkaloids. The subjective symptoms after the consumption of coca turn out to be different for different people. Only a few manifest, as in my case, pure euphoria without any change in condition; others become aware, after the same amounts of cocaine, of signs of light intoxication, the urge to move and talkativeness, while yet others lack all subjective symptoms of the effect of coca. The improvement in capability on the other hand proved to be a far more constant symptom of the effect of coca, and I directed my efforts to demonstrating the latter objectively through the variation in measurements, relating to physical and mental capability, which can easily be determined on living beings. For this purpose I chose to test the strength exerted during a specific action by means of a dynamometer, and to determine the mental reaction time with Exner's *Neuramöbimeter*. As is well known, a dynamometer consists of a springy metal clasp, which pushes a pointer along a graduated arc when it is pressed together, and on which the strength required to press it to-gether to a certain extent can be read in pounds or kilos. Such an instrument can be used, if it is correctly calibrated, and does not require too great an effort in its use, and if, in applying pressure to it, only such an action is performed, as we often carry out with the daily use of our limbs, and the form of which movement is, as it were, already prepared for in our nervous system. The action which I made was pressing with one hand or both hands with outstretched arms, and I soon became convinced that it is very easy to obtain figures which were constant or varied in a constant way with this instrument. The result of my tests was very striking. 0.4 grams of cocaine muriaticum increases the strength of a hand by 2–3 kilos, that of both hands by 3–4 kilos, and what is more this effect occurs after a few minutes at about the same time as the euphoria caused by the coca and subsides gradually over the same period. While conducting such dynamometric measurements I was able to confirm the fact discovered by M. Buch (1884), that muscle strength like temperature reveals a regular diurnal variation. The minimum level of motor capability occurs in the morning after waking up; this rises quickly during the course of the morning, reaching a maximum at midday and declining slowly towards evening. The difference between maximum and minimum in my case amounted to 4 kilos.

I became aware of a second variation in muscle strength, which is independent of the time of day and reveals itself in the fact that on many days one starts with a lower minimum and only attains a lower maximum, so that the diurnal variation occurs on a lower level. The relationship between this reduction in muscle strength and a more depressed general condition was unmistakable to me on each occasion, and it has forced me to the conclusion, that the effect of cocaine occurs not by influencing the motor system but by improving the principal readiness for work. Concerning the effect of cocaine it must also be taken into account that it becomes more noticeable if cocaine is taken when the numbers for motor strength are lower, than if the experiment is conducted when one is in the best condition and at the maximum of one's muscular capability. Determining the mental reaction times led to the same result as the dynamometric tests. As is generally known, by mental reaction time is meant the time which passes between the effect of a sensory impression and the introduction of an arranged motor reaction to it. The time is indicated on Exner's small apparatus in hundredths of seconds by the number of oscillations, which a spring can record on a blackened plate, before it is stopped by the reaction of the person being tested. The sound which arises when the oscillating spring is released serves as a sensory stimulus, which is reacted to. It turned out that my reaction times became shorter and more uniform by the use of cocaine, while they had previously been irregular and extended. On the other hand I obtained just as favourable reaction conditions on other occasions, when I carried out the experiments in the best general state of being without cocaine. In this case as well the relationship between the effect of coca and the euphoria caused by cocaine was evident.

I now come to the two points that are of direct interest for psychiatry. Psychiatry has a wealth of cures that subdue overexcited nervous activity, but on the other hand has a dearth of those that could raise the subdued capability of the nervous system. The idea suggests itself therefore of making use of the effect of cocaine, as has just been described, with those forms of illness which we interpret as states of weakness and depression of the nervous system without any organic lesions. Indeed, since it has become well known, cocaine has been applied in cases of hysteria and hypochondria, etc., and there is no lack of individual reports on cures obtained through its use. Only Morselli and Buccola (1881) have applied it extensively and in a systematic way, and reported that they had achieved some slight improvement. On the whole it has to be said, that the usefulness of cocaine in psychiatric practice still has to be proved and seems to be worth testing carefully, as soon as the exorbitantly priced medication has become inexpensive.

One can talk with greater certainty about another use of cocaine for the psychiatrist. It was in America that the ability of cocaine to reduce the disturbing symptoms which occur during abstinence from morphine in courses of withdrawal treatment and to suppress the craving for morphine was first experienced. The *Detroit Therapeutic Gazette* published a whole series of reports in recent years on morphine and opium withdrawals, which had been conducted with the aid of cocaine. From these, as an example, one can stress the finding that the patients did not require constant medical supervision during the withdrawal, if they were directed to take an effective dose of cocaine whenever the craving for morphine occurred in them again. I myself have had the opportunity of observing a case of morphine withdrawal – indeed a rapid one – under the influence of cocaine, and was able to perceive that the person, who had manifested the most serious symptoms of collapse during a previous withdrawal, was now able to work and did not have to stay in bed, and was only reminded of his abstinence by a feeling of coldness, diarrhoea, and the occasional return of his morphine craving. About 0.40 grams of cocaine were consumed per day, and after twenty days he had fully recovered from his morphine abstinence. An addiction to cocaine did not occur in the process, and on the contrary there was an unmistakable aversion to consuming cocaine. After the experiences I have gathered concerning the effect of cocaine, I would, without giving it a second thought, recommend that one should give cocaine in subcutaneous injections of 0.03–0.05 grams per dose in similar withdrawal cures, and not be afraid of increasing the frequency of the doses.[8] On some occasions I have also noticed, that cocaine quickly removes the symptoms of intolerance which occur after a larger dose of morphine, as though it possessed a specific ability to counteract morphine. Richter, in Pankow, has recently (cf. the *Neurologisches Centralblatt*, of 1 January, 1885) confirmed his experiences concerning the value of cocaine in treating morphine addicts. I am very much aware that cocaine did not seem to help in individual cases of withdrawal cures, and am prepared for the fact that the diversity of individual reactions to the alkaloid will become apparent. Finally I think I should mention, that American doctors have reported curing or favourably influencing the addiction to drink among alcoholics.

Letter to Martha: 2 February, 1886

Paris, Tuesday, 2 February, 1886

My dear sweet Darling,

You write so charmingly and sensibly, and I am reassured every time when you have said what is on your mind. I don't know how I can thank you. Recently I have resolved to show consideration for you in a special way. You will laugh at it: I will try not to be ill. For my tiredness is a kind of slight illness. It's called neurasthenia, which has arisen from the troubles, cares and agitations of recent years, and it has always disappeared from me as if by a stroke of magic, whenever I was with you. So it follows from this, that I must strive to be with you a lot as soon as possible, and as there is no other way for this to happen, except by our getting married, that I must endeavour, to acquire soon that famous three thousand guilders a year. And as I do not lack diligence, and the prospects are not bad, I am also not unhappy and do not worry about my nervousness.

I'm very pleased, that you can testify, that I had thought of the business with the honorarium. I was taken in by it really not through thoughtlessness but from noble-mindedness. There is really nothing more to be said, my Sweet, than what you have said. That is, we are young and have to pay our study fees. I haven't had an answer to my letter to the book dealer yet. I was ashamed at first, of writing to you about the business, and I couldn't refrain from doing so, only because it really did annoy me.

The news of the day is a very friendly letter from Obersteiner, by whose good will I set, as you know, some hope, albeit with a goal which is still vague. He informs me for example about what kind of scientific scandals are happening in Vienna. Just remembering the Vienna circle of highly decent people has a good effect on me. One should not become as bad as people want to make you out to be, but just be careful. The occasion of the letter was that he wants information on the statutes of the Society of Physicians here, which I'll probably be able to provide him with this very evening. Because it's six o'clock and at half-past nine I'm going, as you know, to visit Charcot, not without some dread that I shall enjoy myself very poorly tonight. The preparations were of course much less than on the first occasion, and yet I was in such a bad state, that I could not do any work.

The little bit of cocaine which I have taken makes me talkative, my little woman. I'll continue writing and go into your criticism of my poor self. Do you realise how strangely a person's character is made up, and that his virtues often provide the seed of his destruction and his mistakes bring him happiness? What you write about the character of the Bernays is quite right. But I have no reason to moan about it. It's to this exaggeration, which you yourself so charmingly admit to, that I owe my happiness, for I would never otherwise have found the courage, to woo you. Whether it also means happiness for you, we won't go into. But whoever asks me how things were for me, if all my experiences should come to an end today, will hear me say, that in spite of everything – poverty, slow rates of success, little favour with other people, enormous sensitivity, nervousness and worries – I was happy, through the mere expectation of possessing you and through the certainty that you love me. I was always honest to you, wasn't I? I have not even made use of the freedom that one is usually allowed towards a person of the opposite sex, to present the best side of oneself. I have pointed things out about you and reproached you for a very long time, and the result is that I wish nothing else but to have you, and to have you as you are.

Do you really think that my appearance is so agreeable? You know, I very much doubt it. I think there is something strange about me, and the basic reason for it is that in my youth I was not really young, and now, as the age of maturity begins,

I cannot really age. There was a time, when I was dominated by the desire for knowledge and full of ambition, and I plagued myself day after day with the thought, that Nature had not, in a kind mood, stamped my face with genius, which she sometimes gives generously. Since then I have long known that I am not a genius and no longer understand how I could have wanted to be. I am not even very gifted. All my ability for work is probably to be found in my qualities of character and in the lack of exceptional intellectual weaknesses. I know however, that this mixture is very favourable to gradual success, and that in favourable circumstances I could achieve more than Nothnagel, to whom I believe I am far superior, and that I could perhaps reach the level of Charcot. That does not mean that I will, because I cannot find these favourable conditions any more, and I don't possess genius, the power of bringing them about by force. But how I am chattering on! I wanted to say something completely different, to explain in fact, where my inadequacy and the curtness towards strangers, which you mention, come from. It is only a result of distrust, after my frequent experience, that common or bad people treat me badly, and it will fade away to the extent that I have nothing to fear from them, and as I become stronger and more independent. I console myself with the fact that people who are subordinate to me or at the same level have never felt me to be unpleasant. Only those above me or otherwise superior to me have felt it. You wouldn't think it to look at me, but already at school I always took up a position of fearless opposition, and was always to be found expressing an extreme view and as a rule having to pay for it. Then when, as top of the class for many years, I gained a favoured position, when I was generally trusted, they had nothing to complain about concerning me anymore. Do you know what Breuer said to me one evening? I was so moved by it that I immediately told him the secret concerning our engagement. He said he had discovered that hiding behind my veil of shyness there was an extremely bold and fearless person. I always believed this to be true, but just never had the courage to tell anyone. I often felt, as if I had inherited all the defiance and all the passion of our ancestors, when they defended their temple, and as though I could give up my life with pleasure for one great moment. And yet I was always so powerless and couldn't lend expression to burning passions, even through a word or a poem. So I have always suppressed myself, and I think that's what people notice in me.

I make such stupid confessions to you, my sweet Darling, and actually quite without any reason, unless it is the cocaine, which makes me talk. But now I will go down to dinner, then get dressed and write some more. Tomorrow I will write you a completely truthful account of how the evening at the Charcots turned out. Anyway you should report that I had a splendid time, and I will say the same when I write to Vienna. The truth is just for us alone.

Half-past midnight

Thank God, it's over, and I can report to you straight away, how right I was. Everyone was as stiff as leather, as though they were about to burst, and only the little bit of cocaine protected me from it. Just imagine: forty to fifty people this time, of whom I knew only three or four. No one was introduced to anyone else, and everyone was left to his own devices, to do what he wanted. Of course there was nothing I could do, and I don't think that the others enjoyed themselves any better, but at least they were able to talk. I spoke even worse than usual. No one was concerned about me or could be concerned about me. All that's the normal way things are, and I was prepared for everything. I bowed in front of Madame. She probably did not expect to get much joy out of me and told me that her husband was in the other room. The old man was not very active, and mainly sat in his chair and seemed to me to be very tired. Of course he did not fail to utter little requests now and then, to take this or that, and that was all I got from him. Mademoiselle was wearing a Greek costume, and looked very nice, and I can tell you about this, as your jealousy will not have lasted long. She gave me her hand when I arrived but otherwise did not speak a word to me. Only near the end I got into a political discussion with Giles de la Tourette, during which of course he prophesied that there would be the most furious war with Germany. I revealed myself to be a 'juif', who was neither German nor Austrian. But such conversations are always very embarrassing for me, as I feel something German stirring in me, which I have long decided to suppress. – Getting on for half past eleven we were required to go into the dining room, where there was a lot to eat and drink. I took a cup of chocolate. – You should not think that I am disappointed, as you can't expect anything else from a 'jour fixe',9 and I only know that we won't organise one. But don't tell anyone about how boring it was. We should always tell people about the first evening.

And now Goodnight, my Darling, with warm greetings from
Your Sigmund

Letter to Martha: 10 February, 1886

... On the following day I could not help thinking, what an ass I am to leave Paris, now just as spring is coming, with *Notre Dame* standing there so beautiful in the sunlight, and I only have to mention it to Charcot, to be able to do whatever I want with the patients. But I lack the recklessness and courage to stay here longer.

On the following day, in other words yesterday, Wednesday, another adventure occurred. The Viennese, a very nasty chap, came to fetch me, and we went together to the Salpêtrière. The man is an empty-headed braggart working with Winternitz, and so considers himself to be a great neuropathologist and uttered all kind of expressions of sympathy, which I put up with in the knowledge that revenge was at hand. For he had a letter of re-commendation to Charcot full of exaggerated flattery, such as that he had come to take a look at the greatest living doctor. In response to this he expected to receive God knows what kind of reception, but I knew however that it would be a really cool one. And indeed, as he handed over the letter, Charcot said nothing but 'À votre service, Monsieur,' and added: 'Vous connaissez M. Freud?' whereupon he, taken aback, lowered his head, and I, with inward contentment, lowered mine. Then something else happened. For the last week a stranger has been there, definitely a German type, but somehow a little different, and I didn't know what to make of him. Wednesday is the day we go into the eye treatment room, and there this stranger suddenly made his ap-pearance in an authoritative way, and when he exchanged name cards with Charcot's eye specialist, the latter became very polite and expressed the hope that Monsieur would be coming to visit them often, so that he could profit from his knowledge. This caused us to become inquisitive to find out who he might be. As he left he came up to us two Viennese and said: 'I heard you speaking German. I'd like to introduce myself.' The other man with me was the first to exchange cards with him, and I was still searching for mine, when the stranger said: 'I am a German, but emigrated to America a long time ago.' Finally I gave him my card, but one without a title or address. He threw a glance at it and said: 'Would you be Dr Freud from Vienna? I've long known him from his works, and especially the one on cocaine.' I was rather surprised and asked him his name, which he told me was 'Knapp'. Now Knapp is the leading eye specialist in New York, who has also written a lot about cocaine, and to whom I once sent a letter on Koller's behalf. I greeted him in an appropriate way, and my Viennese colleague stood there very much taken aback, firstly at having failed to recognise the man, and secondly, because in his haste he had made a fool of himself again. When he heard cocaine mentioned, he asked: 'So have you also worked on cocaine?' and Knapp replied: 'Of course, it was he who made it known.' This morning my Viennese colleague was much more accommodating and could speak only of the great medical practice that awaited me in Vienna...

'Remarks on Cocaine Addiction and the Fear of Cocaine', 1887

With reference to a lecture by W.A. Hammonds

The brilliant use to which Karl Koller realised that the anaesthetising characteristic of cocaine could be put, in healing the sick and in improving medical skills, caused the fact to be forgotten for some time that a noteworthy role for the new medication had been claimed in the therapy of internal and nervous illnesses. But among these applications of cocaine, which I can trace back to my work 'On Coca', published in the *Centralblatt für Therapie*, in July 1884, *one* later won the general attention of doctors. I refer to the usefulness of cocaine in fighting the craving for morphine and the disturbing symptoms of collapse, which appear in morphine addicts during the withdrawal cure. I had drawn attention to this characteristic of cocaine according to American reports (in the *Detroit Therapeutic Gazette*) and at the same time reported on the surprisingly favourable course of the first morphine withdrawal treatment undertaken on this continent. (It is perhaps not unnecessary to add the remark, that in this case it was not a matter of an experience with my own body, but advice which I conveyed to another person.)

Prof. H. Obersteiner took the same observation as the occasion for reporting on the effectiveness of cocaine in morphine withdrawal to the doctors who had gathered for the congress in Copenhagen. But he did not make much of an impression. It was not until the circular sent round by the chemical factory of E. Merck in Darmstadt and a constantly enthusiastic essay by Wallé in the *Deutsche Medizinalzeitung* (No. 3, 1885), that the new application of cocaine was brought to the general attention of doctors – and unfortunately also morphine addicts.

There then followed a very energetic rebuttal on the part of Erlenmeyer (in his *Centralblatt* in 1885), which author denied the usefulness of cocaine in a morphine withdrawal cure on the basis of his sequence of experiments with its impressive set of figures, and he also presented it as a dangerous substance due to its effect on the innervation of blood vessels. But Erlenmeyer's conclusions were based nevertheless on a gross experimental error, which was immediately exposed by Obersteiner (1885), Smidt and Rank (1885) and others. Instead of administering, according to my advice, effective doses (of several decigrams) *per os*, Erlenmeyer had given minimal amounts as subcutaneous injections and thus obtained a fleeting toxic effect from an administration which would have been ineffective in the long run. The authors who refuted him were for their part able to provide a complete confirmation of my original reports.

The value of cocaine for morphine addicts was lost for other reasons. The patients themselves began to get hold of the substance and submit it to the same abuse which they used to indulge in with morphine; cocaine should serve them as a substitute for morphine and must really have proved to be an insufficient substitute, as most of the morphine addicts quickly attained enormous doses of one gram per day by subcutaneous injection. It turned out that, used in such a way, cocaine is a much more dangerous threat to health than morphine. Instead of a slow marasmus there is a rapid physical and moral decline, and there are agitated states of hallucination as with alcoholic delirium, as well as chronic persecution mania, which from our experience acquires a characteristic quality in the form of the hallucination of little creatures in the skin, and a craving for cocaine takes the place of a craving for morphine. All these are the sad results of trying to replace one evil by another. Many morphine addicts, who had been able to survive socially, now succumbed to the cocaine. Erlenmeyer, who was able to continue stirring up opposition to the new alkaloid more successfully with his first publications than he had been able to at the beginning, talked of a third scourge of humanity, which was more terrible than the first two (alcohol and morphine).

As at about the same time the first reports about the toxic effects of cocaine consumption were being made by eye and laryngitis specialists, cocaine acquired the reputation of being a highly dangerous substance, the use of which over longer periods generally elicits a form of 'addiction', a 'condition similar to morphine addiction'. I have just found such a warning in the most recent publication on cocaine (by O. Chiari, in the present weekly publication, edition no. 8).

I believe that is going too far. I cannot suppress an obvious remark, which will have the effect of stripping the so-called third scourge of humanity, as Erlenmeyer describes cocaine in such emotive language, of its terror again. *All reports about the addiction and decline caused by cocaine refer to morphine addicts*, people who had already fallen prey to one demon, and who, because of their weakened will-power and need for excitement, would abuse the stimulant offered to them and indeed did abuse it. *In our work cocaine has claimed no other victims, none of its own.* I have many different experiences of the use of cocaine over longer periods by persons who are not morphine addicts, and have taken the medication myself over several months, without feeling or experiencing any kind of special state similar to morphine addiction or desire for further use of cocaine. On the contrary, there occurred, more frequently than I would have liked, an aversion to the medication, which caused me to cease using it. My experiences of the usefulness of cocaine in certain nervous conditions and on the absence of cocaine addiction coincide so completely with the reports, which a well-known foreign authority, W. Hammond, has recently made in reference to the matter, that I prefer to translate Hammond's comments, instead of repeating my findings reported in the work 'On Coca' (*Centralblatt für Therapie*, 1884) and in the later essay ('A Contribution to Knowledge about the Effect of Coca', in the *Wiener Medizinische Wochenschrift*, No. 5, 1885). I would just like to add a few remarks beforehand on the acute cocaine intoxications, which have been observed by eye and laryngitis specialists.

In part these are certainly only states of collapse, as occur after every operation, especially on sensitive parts of the body, and can hardly be attributed to the alkaloid which is often used in minimal amounts. Another sequence of observations, however, unquestionably displays the characteristics of cocaine intoxication due to the symptoms which occur, and which can be produced experimentally by the introduction of an enormous dose of cocaine into the body: these symptoms are numbness as in a state of drunkenness, dizziness, an increase in the pulse rate, a change in breathing, loss of appetite and removal of the need for sleep, to be followed by states of delirium and weakness of the muscles. Such conditions, undoubtedly caused by the cocaine, have sometimes occurred after absorption by the mucous membranes in the head, and at other times, indeed more frequently, after subcutaneous injection. In relation to the frequency of the use of cocaine in the last two years these can be characterised as rare events, and in no case have they become life-threatening. They have therefore quite rightly given most doctors the impression that the possible toxic effects of cocaine do not need to prevent the use of the substance to attain serious goals in operative surgery. An important fact is that such intoxications occur with small doses of cocaine, so that the sensitivity of individual persons to cocaine, together with the fact of the absence of any reaction after larger doses in other persons, has come to be described as completely idiosyncratic.[10] I now believe that this unreliable quality of cocaine, the fact, that is, that one does not know when a toxic effect will occur, is closely related to another, which one must criticise it for possessing, namely that one does not really know when and in whom one can expect it to have an effect in any case (I leave out of consideration of course the anaesthetising effect). The context which makes it easier for us to understand this peculiarity is probably the following: cocaine has quite an obvious effect in irritating the nerves of the blood vessels. In its local application, it causes vascular constriction, that is ischaemia of the tissue. According to B. Fränkel (Discussion at the Berlin Medicinal Society on 4 November, 1885), cocaine causes vascular expansion on the tongue of a frog treated with curare, and only causes vascular constriction in dilution of 1:20,000. According to Erlenmeyer cocaine already has a paralysing effect on the vascular centres and reduces arterial tension when injected in doses of 0.005 grams. According to Litten (see the Discussion etc., 1885), it has an exquisite toning effect, raising the blood pressure. I could cite a whole further sequence of such reports by various researchers, and which sound contradictory, but from all of which one thing stands out, that cocaine has an effect on blood vessels, and, what is more, in various ways according to its concentration, how it is introduced, and the nature of the subject. I must add to this the observation that the description of acute cocaine intoxication sometimes indicates a condition of vascular constriction, and at others one of vascular paralysis. The variable factor, on which the irregular effect of the cocaine depends, seems to me therefore to consist in the condition prevailing at the time and in the delicate condition of the innervation of the blood vessels. I consider it unquestionable that the excitability of the vascular nerves (or vascular nerve centres) is very different in different people and also varies within the individual. The delicate condition of the innervation of the vessels in the brain is probably one of the main symptoms of a nervous condition. One only has to think of the different effects of galvanisation on the back, according to whether it is carried out on a healthy person or a nervous person of one kind or another. Similarly, cocaine, if its general effect is caused by influencing the circulation in the brain, will, on one occasion, be ineffective when there is stable vascular tension, and on another cause a toxic effect by a rapidly occurring fluctuation, while in other cases it will have a strong toning and heightening effect. I suspect therefore the following: *The reason for the irregularity of the effect of cocaine is to be found in the variation in individual excitability and in the variety of conditions of the vascular nerves, on which cocaine exerts its effect.*

As the reason for this excitability is not generally known, and little attention has been paid at all to this factor of individual disposition, I consider it advisable to refrain as far as possible from offering cocaine in the form of subcutaneous injection in the treatment of internal and nervous illnesses.

W. Hammond expressed the following views on cocaine at the sitting of the New York Neurological Society, on 2 November, 1886.*

He employed a coca wine prepared according to his own instructions, which contained two grains[11] of cocaine hydrochloride to one pint of wine, and using this conducted numerous experiments on himself and others. This coca preparation brought about excellent effects on so-called spinal irritation, and these were effects which he could not ascribe to the wine alone. He also found it useful as a tonic and in providing relief from tiredness; for a period of time he himself used to take a wineglass full after the arduous tasks of the day and felt refreshed every time, without having to suffer any depression after it.

He had also applied the preparation in a few cases of dyspepsia in which the stomach was highly sensitive and observed that it had a conspicuously soothing effect. He gave it in doses of two to three teaspoons every fifteen to twenty minutes up to about the sixth dose. The first spoonfuls were generally brought up, but the following ones were always retained for a longer period, until finally the vomiting ceased. Cases of sensitivity of the stomach, which were probably related to spinal irritation (neurasthenia), were found to have been relieved after a few hours of this treatment.

Dr Hammond then touched shortly upon the physiological effects of coca and commented, that the first writers who had reported about its use among the natives of South America, had exaggerated the harmfulness of taking it. Their reports were always rehashed later again and again without citing their

* Reproduced with many abridgements.

sources and thus aroused the prejudice that prevails nowadays. In order to test the horrifying reports on the effect of cocaine, which have filled the newspapers recently, he injected himself repeatedly with cocaine, the slightly toxic effect of which he describes in detail. He did not succumb to any cocaine addiction however, and was able to give up the substance whenever he wanted. Concerning the so-called cocaine addiction, he reports that he has given the substance to a woman suffering from Graves' disease in doses of from 1 to 5 grams over three months. Nevertheless, she was able to give it up without difficulty. He also gave it over several months to a woman addicted to morphine, as a subcutaneous injection of up to 5 grams per day. In this way he was able to overcome the morphine addiction, and the patient did not succumb to cocaine addiction. With all these patients, as with himself, the cocaine produced an exceptional increase in the action of the heart, a raising of the blood pressure and temperature, outbreaks of sweating and sleeplessness.

In three cases of melancholy in women, who refrained from speaking, he succeeded in getting them to speak by injecting them with cocaine, which on some occasions proved to be definitely useful.

Dr Hammond puts the habit of using cocaine on the same level as the habit of drinking coffee or tea; but it is completely different to morphine addiction. He does not believe that there is one single confirmed case of cocaine addiction (except among morphine addicts), of the kind in which the patients are incapable of abandoning the medication whenever they wish. If someone were to take cocaine over a long period of time, then one would expect damage to the heart rather than to any other organs.

The Dream of 'Irma's Injection', July, 1895 (published in *The Interpretation of Dreams,* 1900)

Preface

In the summer of 1895 I had been treating a young woman through psychoanalysis, who was a very close friend to me and my family. It can be understood that such a mingling of relationships can be the source of many different kinds of disturbance for the doctor, especially for the psychotherapist. The personal interest of the doctor is greater, and his authority less. A failure would threaten to loosen the friendship with the relatives of the patient. The treatment ended with partial success: the patient lost her hysterical anxiety, but not all her somatic symptoms. At that time I was not yet really sure about the criteria, which would denote that the case history of an hysteric had been finally concluded, and I asked the patient to accept a solution, which did not seem acceptable to her. In this state of disagreement we broke off the treatment because it was the summer period. One day a younger colleague, one of my closest friends, visited me. He had visited the patient – Irma – and her family at their country residence. I asked him how he had found her, and the answer I received was: she is better, but not completely well. I know that the words of my friend Otto, or the tone, in which they were uttered, annoyed me. I thought I could detect some reproach, such as that I had promised the patient too much, and I traced – whether rightly or wrongly – the fact, as I thought, that Otto was taking sides against me, to the influence of the patient's relatives, who, as I assumed, had not looked favourably on my treatment. Incidentally I did not understand my embarrassing feeling, nor did I express it in any way. The same evening I wrote down Irma's case history, in order to give it, as though justifying myself, to Dr M., a common friend, and one of the prominent figures in our circle at that time. During the night following this evening (probably more during the morning after), I had the following dream, which was set down immediately after waking.*

The Dream of 23–4 July, 1895

A large hall – many guests, whom we are receiving – Among them is Irma, whom I immediately take aside, in order, as it were, to answer her letter, and to make reproaches to her, that she had still not accepted my 'solution'. I say to her: If you still have pains, then it is really only your own fault. She replies: If you knew, what kinds of pains I have now in my throat, stomach and body, it's constricting me. I am startled and look at her. She looks pale and bloated, and I think that perhaps after all I am overlooking some organic problem. I take her to the window and look into her throat. She shows some resistance while I am doing so, as women do who wear a set of false teeth. I think to myself that she does not need to do this. The mouth then opens fully, and I find a large white patch on the right and elsewhere extensive greyish-white scabs on some remarkable wrinkled shapes, which are obviously made like nasal concha. I quickly call out to Dr M., who repeats the examination and confirms my findings... Dr M looks completely different from the way he usually does: he is very pale, limps, and has no beard on his chin... My friend Otto is now also standing next to her, and my friend Leopold conducts a percussive examination of her over her bodice and says: She has an attenuation down on the left, and he indicates an infiltrated patch of skin on her left shoulder (which I can feel as he can despite her dress)... M. says: There's no doubt about it, it's an infection, but it doesn't matter; it will be followed by some dysentery and the poison will be expelled... We also know immediately where the infection comes from. Our friend Otto

* [Added in 1914] This is the first dream, which I subjected to a thorough interpretation.

gave her an injection not long ago, when she was feeling unwell, with a preparation of propyl, propyl… propionic acid… trimethylamine (the formula for which I see printed in bold before me)… Such injections should not be made rashly… Probably the needle also wasn't clean.

This dream has one advantage over many others. It is immediately clear to which events of the previous day it relates and what theme it deals with. The preface has provided information about this. The news, which I received from Otto about Irma's condition, and the case history, which I had been writing up until late at night, occupied my mental activity during my sleep as well. Nevertheless no one, who has knowledge of the preface and the content of the dream, could imagine what the dream signifies. I myself do not know. I am surprised at the symptoms of the illness about which Irma complains to me in the dream, as they are not the same as those for which I have been treating her. I smile at the absurd idea of an injection of propionic acid, and the words of consolation which Dr M. utters. The dream seems to me to become darker and more condensed towards its end than it is at the beginning. To discover the meaning of all this, I must decide on a detailed analysis.

Analysis

The hall – many guests, whom we receive. During that summer we were living in Bellevue, a house which stands on its own on one of the hills, which are connected to the Kahlenberg. This house had been formally intended as a place of entertainment, and has the unusually high rooms like halls of such establishments. The dream also occurred in the Bellevue, and indeed a few days before my wife's birthday. On the day before, my wife had expressed the hope, that several friends, among them also Irma, would be our guests. Thus my dream anticipates this situation: it is my wife's birthday, and many people, including

Irma, are being received by us as guests in the great hall of Bellevue.

I make reproaches to Irma, that she has not accepted the solution. I say: If you still have pains, it is your own fault. I could have said that to her when awake, or have actually said it. I was then of the opinion (later recognised as incorrect), that my task did not go beyond conveying the hidden meaning of their symptoms to the patients; I am no longer responsible for whether they accept this solution or not, on which success depends. I am thankful to this error, now happily overcome, for having made my existence easier at a time when, in all my inevitable ignorance, I expected to produce successful cures. I notice however, that in the sentence which I speak to Irma in the dream, I want above all not to be responsible for the pains which she still has. If it is Irma's own fault, then it cannot be mine. Perhaps it is in this direction that one should seek the purpose of the dream?

Irma's complaints: pains in the throat, body and stomach, feelings of constriction. Stomach pains were part of my patient's complex of symptoms, but were not a matter of any urgency; she complained rather about feelings of nausea and disgust. Pains in the throat, the body, and constriction of the gullet hardly played any role in her case. I am surprised why I decided on this choice of symptoms in the dream, and cannot find an answer for the moment.

She looks pale and bloated. My patient always had a rosy complexion. I suspect that another person has been imposed upon her.

I am startled at the thought, that I have after all overlooked some organic affection. It will be readily believed when I say that this is a source of incessant anxiety for the specialist, who deals exclusively with neurotics and who is used to attributing so many symptoms to hysteria, which other doctors treat as organic. On the other hand, a faint doubt creeps over me – I do not know where it comes from – whether my being startled is completely genuine. If Irma's pains are organically based, then on the other hand I have no obligation to cure them. My treatment only gets rid of hysterical pains. It actually seems to me therefore, that I should wish for some error in the diagnosis: then the reproach of failure would also be disposed of.

I take her to the window to look down her throat. She shows some resistance, as women do who wear a set of false teeth. I think to myself that she does not need to do this. In Irma's case I never had cause to inspect the oral cavity. The event in the dream reminds me of the examination conducted some time ago of a governess, who had at first given the impression of youthful beauty, but who, on opening her mouth, made some attempt to conceal her set of teeth. There are associations between this case and other memories of medical examinations and little secrets which are revealed during them, giving no pleasure to either party involved. – *She does not need to do this*, is in the first place surely a compliment for Irma, but I suspect that there is also another meaning. In an attentive analysis one feels whether one has exhausted or not the expected hidden thoughts. The way in which Irma is standing by the window reminds me suddenly of another experience. Irma has an intimate lady friend, for whom I have very high regard. When I paid a visit on her one evening, I found her in the situation by the window as reproduced in the dream, and her doctor, that same Dr M., explained that she had a coating typical of diphtheritis. This figure, Dr M., and the coating recur in the subsequent part of the dream. Now it occurs to me, that in the last few months I have had every reason to assume that this other woman is also a hysteric. Indeed, Irma herself revealed this fact to me. But what do I know about her circumstances? Just the one thing, that she suffers from a hysterical choking condition like my Irma does in the dream. In the dream I have thus replaced my patient by her friend. Now I remember that I have often toyed with the suspicion, that this woman might likewise make demands on me, to free her of her symptoms. But then I considered it unlikely, for she has a very reserved nature. She *shows resistance*, as is shown in the dream. Another explanation would be *that she does not need to do this*; she has really shown herself hitherto to be strong enough, to control her condition without the help of anyone else. Now there only remain a few details, which I can attribute to neither Irma nor her friend: *pale, bloated, false teeth.* The false teeth led me back to that governess, and I felt inclined to be satisfied with *bad* teeth. Then another person occurs to me, to whom those details could allude. She is also not my patient, and I would not like to have her as a patient, as I have noticed that she feels embarrassed in front of me and I do not consider her to be a compliant patient. She is usually pale, and once when it was an especially good time for her she was bloated.* So I have compared my patient with two other people, who would likewise resist treatment. What can be the meaning of the fact that I have switched her with her friend in the dream? Most likely that I would like to switch them: the other woman either awakens stronger feelings of sympathy or I have a higher opinion of her intelligence. I consider Irma in fact to be unwise, because she does not accept my solution. The other would have been cleverer and would have been more likely to yield. *The mouth then opens fully*: She would tell more than Irma did.[†]

What I see in the throat: a white patch and nasal concha with scabs. The white patch reminds me of diphtheritis and thus of Irma's friend, but also of the serious illness of my eldest daughter about

* The still unexplained complaint about *pains in the body* can also be traced to this third person. The person in question is of course my own wife; the body pains remind me of one occasion, on which her shyness became clear to me. I have to admit to myself, that I do not treat Irma and my wife in a very kind way in this dream, but it must be said in my excuse, that I am judging both against the ideal of the good, compliant woman patient.

† I suspect that the interpretation of this part has not been taken far enough to pursue all of the hidden meaning. If I were to continue the comparison of the three women, then I would become too distracted. Every dream has at least one part, in which it becomes unfathomable, just like a navel by which it is connected to the Unknown.

almost two years ago and of the frightening experience of that awful time. The scab on the nasal concha reminds me of some concern about my own health. At that time I frequently used cocaine, to suppress troublesome swellings of the nose, and had heard a few days before, that a woman patient, who did the same thing, had contracted an extensive necrosis of the nasal mucous membrane. The recommendation to use cocaine, which was initiated by me in 1885,[12] has also brought grave accusations against me. A dear friend, who had already died in 1895 (the date of the dream), had hastened his own decline through the abuse of this remedy.

I quickly call out to Dr M., who repeats the examination. That would simply correspond to the position which Dr M. held amongst us...[13] It reminds me of a sad medical experience. I had once, through the continued prescription of a remedy, which was then still considered harmless (sulfonal), caused heavy intoxication in a woman patient, and I turned in all haste to that experienced older colleague for assistance. The fact that I really had this case in mind is substantiated by a secondary circumstance. The patient, who succumbed to the intoxication,[14] bore the same name as my eldest daughter. I had never thought about it until now; now it seems almost like fate taking its revenge. It was as though the substitution of the two people should continue in another sense: this Mathilde for that Mathilde, an eye for an eye, a tooth for a tooth. It is as though I was seeking out all the occasions with which I can reproach myself for a lack of medical conscientiousness.

Dr M. is pale, without a beard on his chin and he limps. That much is true in this case, that his bad appearance often awakens concern among his friends. The two other characteristics must belong to another person. I think of my older brother who lives abroad, and whose chin is shaven, and if I remember correctly, the Dr M. in the dream looked just like him. A few days before some news concerning him had arrived: due to an arthritic affliction in his hip he was limping. There must be a reason why

I merge the two persons together into a single one in the dream. I can actually remember that I had bad feelings about both of them for similar reasons. Both had rejected a certain suggestion which I had made to them recently.

My friend Otto is standing next to the patient, and my friend Leopold examines her and indicates an attenuation down on the left. My friend Leopold is also a doctor, and a relative of Otto. Fate has made rivals of them both, who are constantly compared with each other, as they are specialists in the same field. They both worked as my assistants for several years, when I was head of a public medical service for mentally ill children. Scenes like those reproduced in the dream often took place there. While I was discussing the diagnosis of a case with Otto, Leopold had examined the child again and provided an unexpected contribution to our verdict. There existed a similar difference in character between them as between Inspector Bräsig and his friend Karl.[15] The one distinguished himself by his 'speed', and the other was slow, thoughtful but thorough. If I compare Otto and the careful Leopold in the dream, then this obviously occurs with the intention of emphasising Leopold. It is a similar comparison as that above between the disobedient patient Irma and her friend who is regarded as being cleverer. I now perceive one of the lines which the thought connection in the dream is following: from sick child to the institute for sick children. *The attenuation down on the left* gives me the impression, as though it might correspond to all the details of an individual case, in which Leopold had astonished me by his thoroughness. I also have in mind something like a metastatic affection, but it could also be a connection to the patient, whom I should like to have instead of Irma. This woman simulates in fact, as far as I can assess it, a tubercular condition.

An infiltrated patch of skin on her left shoulder. I know immediately that this is the rheumatism in my own shoulder, which I feel frequently, whenever I have stayed awake till late at night. The wording in the dream also sounds ambiguous in this way: *which I can feel as he can.* This means feeling it on my own body. Incidentally it occurs to me how unusual the description 'infiltrated patch of skin' sounds. We are familiar with the expression 'infiltration up on the left at the back': that would refer to the lung and thus to tuberculosis again.

In spite of her dress. This is only an interpolation however. We naturally examined the children at the institute without their clothes. It is some kind of contrast to the way we have to examine adult woman patients. It used to be said of an outstanding clinician that he always examined his patients physically only through their clothes. The rest is vague to me, and, to be honest, I have no inclination to go into it more deeply.

Dr M. says: it's an infection, but it doesn't matter. It will be followed by some dysentery and the poison will be expelled. This seems ridiculous to me at first, but it must, like everything else, be carefully dissected. When examined more closely, it does reveal a kind of sense. What I had found in the patient was local diphtheritis. From the time when my daughter was ill I remember the discussion about diphtheritis and diphtheria. The latter is the general infection which develops from the local form of diphtheritis. Leopold demonstrates such a general infection by pointing out the attenuation, which makes one think of metastatic origins. I believe however that it is precisely in the case of diphtheria that such forms of metastasis do not occur. They remind me more of pyaemia.

It does not matter. This is a consolation. I think it fits in as follows: the last part of the dream contains the information that the patient's pains are caused by a serious organic affection. I suspect that with this as well I am trying to shift the blame from myself. A mental cure cannot be made responsible for the continuation of diphtheritic sufferings. Now it disturbs me however that I impute such a serious complaint to Irma, solely to exonerate myself. It seems to be so cruel. I need some assurance therefore of a good outcome, and it seems to me not a bad choice to put the expression of consolation into the mouth of Dr M. But I am here going beyond the dream, which requires some explanation. So why is this consolation so ridiculous?

Dysentery: Some sort of remote theoretical idea that patho-genic material can be removed through the bowels. Do I want to make fun of the wealth of Dr M.'s far-fetched explanations of strange pathological associations? Something else occurs to me in connection with dysentery. A few months ago I had taken over the case of a young man who had strange problems with his stool, and whom other colleagues had treated as a case of 'anaemia with malnutrition'. I realised that it was a case of hysteria, but did not want to try out my method of psycho-therapy on him, and sent him on a sea trip. Then a few days ago I received a desperate letter from him from Egypt, stating that there he had suffered a new attack, which the doctor had described as dysentery. I suspect indeed that the diagnosis is only a mistake made by that ignorant colleague, who let himself be fooled by the hysteria. But I could not spare myself the reproaches, that I had put the patient in a position, in which, in addition to his hysterical bowel affection, he had acquired an organic one. In addition dysentery sounds like diphtheria,[16] which is not mentioned by name in the dream.

Yes, it must be the case, that I am making fun of Dr M. with the comforting prognosis: it will be followed by some dysentery, and so on. For I remember that once some years ago he laugh-ingly related something very similar about a colleague. He had been called to a consultation with this colleague in the case of a seriously ill man, and felt obliged to point out to the other doctor, who seemed to be very hopeful, that there was albumen in the urine. The colleague did not let himself be put off how-ever, but answered calmly: *It doesn't matter*, Doctor, *that albumen will soon be expelled*! So I no longer have any doubt that this part of the dream contains an expression of scorn at the colleagues who know nothing about hysteria. As though in confirmation of this the thought now occurs to me: does Dr M. know, that the symptoms of his patient, Irma's friend, which give cause to fear a case of tuberculosis, also have a hysterical basis? Was he able to identify it as hysteria, or was he taken in by her?

But what motive can I have, for treating this friend so badly? It is quite simple: Dr M. is as little in agreement with the 'solution' I proposed to Irma as Irma is herself. So in this dream I have already taken my revenge on two people: on Irma, with my remarks 'If you still have pains, it is your own fault'; and on Dr M., with the wording of absurd consolation that I put into his mouth.

We know immediately where the infection comes from. This immediate knowledge in the dream is strange. Just before that we did not know about it yet, as the infection was first proved by Leopold.

Our friend Otto gave her an injection, when she was feeling unwell. Otto had really mentioned that, in the short time that he was with Irma's family, he had been summoned to a neighbouring hotel, to give an injection to someone there who suddenly felt unwell. The injections remind me again of the unlucky friend, who poisoned himself with cocaine. I had given him the remedy only to be taken internally during withdrawal from morphine, but he promptly gave himself cocaine injections.

With a preparation of propyl... propyl... propionic acid. How do I arrive at that? The same evening, after which I had been writing up the case history and following which I had the dream, my wife opened a bottle of liqueur, on which the word 'Ananas'* could be read and which was a gift of our friend Otto. He had the habit of giving gifts on all possible occasions: it is to be hoped that one day he will be cured of this by a woman.† This

* 'Ananas' is remarkably reminiscent of the family name of my patient Irma. [*Ananas* is the German word for pineapple.]
† [Added in 1909 but omitted in editions after 1925.] In this respect the dream proved not to be prophetic. But in another sense it was proved right, for the 'unsolved' stomach problems of my patient, which I did not want to be responsible for, were the precursors of a severe gallstone complaint.

liqueur emitted such a smell of cheap alcohol that I hesitated to taste it. My wife's opinion was: let's give this bottle to the servants. But I, more cautiously, forbad her to, remarking philanthropically, that they should not poison themselves either. The smell of cheap alcohol (amyl...) obviously awoke in me the whole sequence: propyl, methyl, etc., which provided the propyl preparations in the dream. It is true that I carried out a substitution in the process, dreaming about propyl after I had smelt amyl, but perhaps those kind of substitutions can be allowed, especially in organic chemistry.

Trimethylamine. In the dream I see the chemical formula for this substance, which certainly demonstrates a great effort of memory on my part, and what is more the formula is printed in bold, as though the intention were to make something stand out from the context as especially important. So where does this trimethylamine lead me, to which my attention has been drawn in such a way? To a conversation with another friend, who has known about the germinating process of all my work for many years, as I have about his.[17] At that time he had informed me about certain ideas on a theory of sexual chemistry and mentioned, amongst other things, that he thought he was able to identify one of the products of sexual metabolism as trimethylamine. This substance leads me to sexuality therefore, that factor, to which I attribute the greatest significance in the origin of nervous affections, which I want to cure. My patient Irma is a young widow. If it is my concern to apologise to her for the failure of the cure, then it would be best for me to refer to this fact, which her friends would like to change. How strangely such a dream is constructed! The other woman, whom I have as a patient instead of Irma in the dream, is also a young widow.

I can guess why the formula for trimethylamine has become so prominent in the dream. So many important things come together in this one word: trimethylamine is not only an allusion to the uncontrollable power of sexuality, but also to a person, whose agreement I recall with satisfaction, whenever

I feel desperately alone in my views. Should not this friend, who plays such an important role in my life, occur again in the thought complex of the dream? Indeed, he is a specialist on the effects, which come from nasal affections and paranasal sinuses, and he has contributed knowledge to science about the strange relationships between the nasal concha and female sexual organs (the three wrinkled shapes in Irma's throat). I arranged for Irma to be examined by him, to see if her stomach pains might have a nasal origin. But he himself suffers from nasal abscesses, which worry me, and that is probably what the pyaemia alludes to, which I have in mind in the metastatic aspects of the dream.[18]

Such injections should not be made rashly. Here the reproach of carelessness is flung directly at my friend Otto. I think I thought something similar during the afternoon, when, through his words and the way he looked, he showed that he was taking sides against me. It was as though I were thinking: how easily he lets himself be influenced, how easily he manages to come to a judgement. Apart from that the sentence above refers me again to the friend who died, and who decided so quickly to inject himself with cocaine. As I have already said, I had not intended at all that the substance should be injected. With the reproach, which I make against Otto, of handling chemical substances carelessly, I realise that I am again touching upon the case of that unfortunate Mathilde, from whom the same reproach against myself originates. I am obviously collecting examples here of my conscientiousness, but also of its opposite.

Probably the needle also wasn't clean. Another reproach against Otto, but which comes from somewhere else. Yesterday I met by chance the son of an eighty-two-year-old woman, to whom I have to give two morphine injections every day. She is at present in the countryside, and I heard that she was suffering from phlebitis. I thought immediately that it must be a case of an infiltrate through contamination of the needle. I am proud of the fact that I have not given her a single infiltrate in two years, and I am of course constantly concerned about whether the needle is clean. I am quite simply conscientious. Phlebitis brings me again to my wife, who had suffered from blocked arteries during a pregnancy. So now three similar situations have emerged in my memory, concerning my wife, Irma and the dead Mathilde, and their identical nature have clearly given me the right to substitute the three people for each other in the dream.

I have now completed the analysis of the dream.* During this work I had difficulty avoiding all the ideas which were of necessity stimulated by the comparison between the content of the dream and the dream thoughts hidden behind it. Meanwhile the 'meaning' of the dream has become clear to me. I have noticed an intention, which is realised by the dream and which must have been the motivation for the dream. The dream fulfils some wishes, which have been activated in me by the events of the previous evening (Otto's news, and the writing down of the case history). The result of the dream is in fact to make me not guilty of Irma's suffering, which still persists, but to make Otto guilty of it. Now Otto had annoyed me by his remark about Irma's incomplete cure, and the dream takes revenge on him for me, by turning the reproach back upon himself. The dream acquits me of responsibility for Irma's condition, by attributing it to other factors (a whole series of reasons at the same time). The dream represents certain facts as I would like them to be: *Its content is therefore a wish-fulfilment and its motivation a wish*.

This much is obvious. But many of the details of the dream become comprehensible to me from the perspective of wish-fulfilment. I am taking my revenge on Otto not only for the way

---

* [Added in 1909.] Even if, understandably, I have not communicated everything, which occurred to me in connection with the work of interpretation.

he rashly took sides against me, by attributing to him a rash medical act (the injection), but I am also taking revenge on him for the bad cheap-smelling liqueur, and in the dream I find an expression which combines both reproaches: the injection with a propyl preparation. I am still not satisfied but continue to take my revenge, by contrasting him with his more reliable rival. I seem to be saying by this: I prefer him to you. But Otto is not the only one to feel the force of my anger. I am also revenging myself on the disobedient woman patient, by replacing her with a cleverer more compliant one. I do not let Dr M.'s opposition pass either, but through a clear allusion I express my opinion to him, that he is an ignoramus when confronted by this matter (*It will be followed by some dysentery*, etc.). Yes, it seems to me that I am making an appeal not to him but to another person, who knows better (my friend, who told me about trimethylamine), just as I turned from Irma to her friend, and from Otto to Leopold. Get rid of these people, replace them by three others of my own choosing, and then I will be rid of the reproaches that I don't want to have deserved. The unfounded nature of these reproaches themselves is proven to me most extensively in the dream. Irma's pains are not a burden to me, for she herself is to blame for them, by refusing to accept my solution. Irma's pains do not concern me, for they are organic in nature, and not at all curable by psychological treatment. Irma's pains can be satisfactorily explained by her widowhood (trimethylamine!), which I cannot change in any way. Irma's pains have been caused by a careless injection on the part of Otto using an unsuitable substance, in a way that I would never have done. Irma's suffering has been caused by an injection using a dirty needle like the phlebitis of the old female patient of mine, while I never cause any problems with my injections. Admittedly, I notice that these explanations of Irma's sufferings, which have the common aim of exonerating me, are not in harmony with each other, indeed they contradict each other. The whole plea – for the dream is nothing other than that – reminds one vividly of the defence made by the man who was accused by his neighbour of having returned to him a pot in a defective condition: he claimed that in the first place he had brought it back undamaged, secondly the pot already had a hole in it when he borrowed it, and thirdly he had never borrowed a pot from his neighbour. But so much the better: if only one of these three forms of defence is recognised as valid, then the man must be declared innocent.

Yet other themes contribute to the dream and the relationship of them to my exoneration from guilt for Irma's illness is not so clear: the illness of my daughter and that of the patient of the same name, the harmfulness of cocaine, the affection acquired by my patient who was travelling in Egypt, the concern about the health of my wife, of my brother and of Dr M., my own physical complaints and the concern about my absent friend, who suffers from nasal abscesses. But when I consider all these things, they all fit together into one thought complex, which can be categorised as something like: concern about health, both mine and that of others, and medical conscientiousness. I recall a vague feeling of embarrassment when Otto brought me the news of Irma's condition. I would like to lend expression subsequently to this fleeting feeling from the thought complex which played a role in the dream. It is as though it wanted to say to me: you do not take your medical duties seriously enough, are not conscientious, and do not keep your promises. Consequently, that thought complex had been put at my disposal, so that I could produce proof of how highly conscientious I am, how much I have the health of the members of my family, friends and patients at heart. Remarkably there are also embarrassing memories among this mass of thoughts, which rather provide evidence for the accusation attributed to my friend Otto than for excusing me. The material itself is impartial, but the relationship between this broader subject matter, on which the dream is based, and the narrower theme of the dream from which the wish arose not to be responsible for Irma's illness, is unmistakable.

I do not want to assert that I have revealed the meaning of this dream completely and that its interpretation is comprehensive.

I could dwell on it much longer, draw more enlightenment from it and discuss new puzzles which it throws up. I myself know the points from which further connections between thoughts could be followed. But concerns, such as those which must be considered with every one of one's own dreams, make me refrain from such a work of interpretation. Anyone who is ready to censure me for such reserve should himself try to be franker than I have been. I am satisfied for the moment with the one newly won insight: if the method of dream interpretation indicated here is followed, then it will be found that dreams really do have meaning and are by no means the expression of fragmented mental activity, as other writers would have it. *After the work of interpretation is completed, a dream reveals itself to be a wish-fulfilment.*

From 'Sexuality in the Aetiology of the Neuroses', January and February, 1898

Masturbation occurs much more frequently among grown-up girls and mature men, than is usually accepted, and has a harmful effect not only by creating neurasthenic symptoms, but also by keeping the patients under the pressure of a secret which is felt to be shameful. The doctor who is not used to understanding neurasthenia in terms of masturbation accounts for the sick condition by referring to it with such clichés as anaemia, malnutrition, overwork etc., and then expects to heal the patient by application of the therapy developed against such things. To his surprise periods of improvement in the patient alternate with others, in which all the symptoms become worse with a serious worsening of the state of mind. The outcome of such treatment is generally doubtful. If the doctor knew that the patient was struggling all the time with his sexual habit, and that he had fallen into despair because he had had to succumb to it yet again, and if he understood how to relieve the patient of his secret, to lessen the severity of it in his eyes and to support him in his struggle to give up the habit, then the success of his therapeutic effort would be thereby assured.

Giving up the habit of masturbation is only one of the new therapeutic tasks which arise for the doctor when he takes sexual aetiology into consideration, and it appears that precisely this task, just like giving up habits in all other cases, can only be carried out in a medical institution and under the constant supervision of a doctor. Left to himself, the masturbator tends, whenever his mood is influenced in a bad way, to fall back on the form of satisfaction which is convenient for him. Medical treatment can in this case have no other goal than to direct the neurasthenic, once he has regained his strength in the direction of normal sexual intercourse, for sexual need, once it has been awoken and provided with satisfaction over some considerable time, can no longer be silenced, but only directed a different way. A completely analogous comment would also be valid for all other kinds of cures through abstinence, which will only appear to be successful as long as the doctor is satisfied with taking away the narcotic substance from the patient, without concerning himself about the source from which the imperative need for such things originates. The word 'habit' is a mere expression without any explanatory value: not everyone who has the opportunity to take morphine for a time, cocaine, chloral hydrate and so on, acquires an 'addiction' to these things. Closer examination usually reveals, that these narcotics are usually intended as a substitute, either directly or in a roundabout way, for sexual enjoyment, and where a normal sexual life cannot be restored, then one can with certainty expect the person who has broken with such a habit to suffer a relapse.

The Dream of 'The Botanical Monograph', March 1898 (published in *The Interpretation of Dreams*, 1900)

I have written a monograph on a certain plant. The book lies in front of me, and I am just turning over a coloured plate enclosed in it. A dried specimen of the plant is bound into every copy, just as though it were from a herbarium.

Analysis

During the morning I saw a new book in the display window of a bookshop, which had the title: *The Cyclamen Genus* – obviously a *monograph* on this plant.

Cyclamen is the *favourite flower* of my wife. I reproach myself that I so seldom think of *bringing her flowers*, as she would like me to. The theme of *bringing flowers* reminds me of a story, which I recently told among a circle of friends and used as proof of my assertion, that forgetting is very often the carrying out of an unconscious intention and nevertheless allows one to deduce something about the secret state of mind of the person who forgets. A young woman who was used to finding a bouquet from her husband on her birthday, misses this sign of tenderness on one such anniversary and bursts into tears about it. The husband arrives, and cannot explain her crying to himself, until she says to him: 'Today is my birthday.' He strikes himself on the forehead and exclaims: 'I'm sorry, I completely forgot it,' and wants to go and get her some *flowers*. But she will not be consoled, for she perceives in her husband's forgetfulness proof of the fact, that she does not play the same role in his thoughts as she once did. My wife met this Frau L. two days ago, and was told by her that she felt well, and she asked after me. Some years ago she was treated by me.

A new approach: I really did write something once which was similar to a *monograph* on a plant, in fact my essay on the *Coca Plant* (1884), which drew K. Koller's attention to the anaesthetising characteristic of cocaine. I had myself indicated this application of the alkaloid in my publication, but had not been sufficiently thorough to pursue the matter further. In connection with this it occurs to me, that during the morning after the dream (for the interpretation of which I could not find any time until the evening) I thought about cocaine in a kind of daydream. If ever I contracted glaucoma, I would travel to Berlin and have myself operated on incognito at the home of my Berlin friend (Fliess) by a doctor, recommended by him. The man doing the operation, who would not know on whom he was working, would praise yet again the fact that these types of operations had proved to be so easy since the introduction of cocaine. I would not betray by any facial expression that I myself played a role in this discovery. Other thoughts became associated with this fantasy, such as how awkward it is for a doctor to make demands on the medical accomplishments of his colleagues for his own needs. I would be able to pay the Berlin eye specialist, who does not know me, as anyone else would. Only after this daydream has come into my mind, do I notice that the memory of a particular event is hidden behind it. Shortly after Koller's discovery, my father had in fact contracted glaucoma; he was operated on by my friend, the eye specialist, Dr Königstein. Dr Koller took care of the anaesthesia using cocaine and then remarked that in this case all three people had been brought together who had played a part in the introduction of cocaine.

My thoughts then turn to when I was last reminded of this story about cocaine. It was a few days ago, when I received the commemorative volume, with the publication of which grateful students had celebrated the anniversary of their teacher and of the governing board of the laboratory. Among the laboratory's claims to fame I also found it mentioned that the discovery of the anaesthetising effect of cocaine had occurred there. I now suddenly realise that my dream is connected to an experience of the evening before. I had just accompanied Dr Königstein home and had got involved in a conversation with him about a matter, which always gets me worked up in a lively way when it is touched upon. While I was standing with him in the entrance hall, Professor *Gärtner* joined us with his young wife. I could not refrain from congratulating both of them on the fact that they were *blooming* with health. Now Professor Gärtner is the author of the commemorative volume, which I have just mentioned, and could well have reminded me of this. And Frau L., about whom I had recently told the story of the disappointment on her birthday, had also been mentioned in the conversation with Dr Königstein, though in connection with something else.

I will try to interpret the other distinctive elements of the dream content. A *dried specimen* of the plant is enclosed with the monograph, as though it were a *herbarium*. The herbarium reminds me of a memory of my grammar school days. Our headmaster summoned the pupils of the higher classes together, to give them the job of checking and cleaning out the school's herbarium. Small *worms* had been found there – bookworms.[19] He does not seem to have had any trust in my assistance, for he let me have only a few leaves. I still remember now that there were cruciferae on them. I never had an especially close knowledge of botany. In my preliminary examination in botany I was again given a crucifera to identify and – I did not recognise it. It would have gone badly for me if my theoretical knowledge had not helped me out. From the crucifera I come to the compositae. Actually the artichoke is also a composita, and in fact what I could call *my favourite flower*. Being more magnanimous than me, my wife has the habit of bringing me home this favourite flower of mine from the market.

I see the monograph, which I have written, *lying in front of me*. This is also not without some connection. My friend, who is visually oriented (Fliess), wrote to me yesterday from Berlin: 'I am devoting myself a great deal to thoughts about your book on dreams. *I see it lying finished in front of me and I am turning over its pages.*' How I envied him this gift of prophecy! If only I could also see it lying finished in front of me!

The folded coloured plate:[20] When I was a medical student, I suffered greatly from the impulse, to want to learn only from *monographs*. In those days I obtained, despite my limited means, several medical archive works, the coloured plates in which were a delight to me. I was proud of this tendency to thoroughness. When I myself started to publish things, I had to draw the plates for my treatises, and I know that one of them turned out so miserably that a well-wishing colleague mocked me because of it. There also occurs to me, I don't know how I got to it, a memory from my early years. My father once thought it a good joke to let me and my oldest sister have a book with coloured plates (the description of a journey in Persia) to tear apart. This could hardly be justified educationally. I was five years old at the time, and my sister less than three years old, and the image of us children overjoyed at pulling this book apart[21] (*like an artichoke, leaf by leaf,*[22] I should add), is almost the only one, which I have retained as a vivid memory of that time in my life. When I became a student, I developed a definite liking for collecting and possessing books (analogous to the inclination to study using monographs, a *favourite thing,*[23] as already occurs in the dream concerning cyclamen and artichokes). I became a *bookworm* (Cf. *herbarium*). I have always, since I started to think about myself, traced this first passion of my life back to that impression made on me as a child, or rather I have realised, that this childhood scene is a 'screen memory'* for my later love of books. Of course I also had the experience early that passions easily lead one into suffering. When I was seventeen years old, I had a considerable account with the book dealer and no means of settling it, and my

---

* Compare my essay 'On Screen Memories'.

father did not consider it a valid excuse, that my inclinations had not been directed towards anything more wicked. Mentioning this later experience from my youth brings me back immediately to the conversation with my friend Dr Königstein however. For in the conversation on the evening of the day when I had the dream, there was also mention of the same reproaches as at that time in the past, that I give in too much to my *favourite things*.

For reasons which are not relevant to mention here, I will not pursue the interpretation of this dream any further, but merely indicate the path which leads to it. During the work of interpretation I was reminded of the conversation with Dr Königstein, and indeed starting from more than one point. When I consider what matters were touched on in this conversation, the meaning of the dream becomes comprehensible to me. All the trains of thought which had been taken up, the favourite things of my wife and myself, cocaine, the difficulties of medical treatment amongst colleagues, my liking of studies in the form of monographs and my neglect of certain fields such as botany, all these are continued and lead to one of the threads of the many-branched discourse. Again the dream acquires the character of a justification, a plea that I am in the right, like the dream of Irma's injection which was analysed first. Indeed it continues with the same theme as in that case and discusses it using new material, which has appeared in the interval between the two dreams. Even the apparently indifferent form of expression used by the dream is emphasised. The meaning this time is: I am indeed the man who wrote the valuable and successful treatise (on cocaine), just as in the previous case I justified myself by saying: I am a competent and diligent student. In both cases therefore it is saying: I can allow myself to do something. I can however refrain from carrying out the interpretation of the dream in this context, because I was only motivated to report this dream, in order to examine, by reference to an example, the connection between the dream content and the experience of the previous day which stimulated it. As long as I only know the manifest content of this dream, then only one connection between the dream and one impression of the day before will be obvious. After I have made the analysis, a second source of the dream arises in another experience of the same day. The first of the impressions to which the dream refers is a trivial one, a secondary fact. I see a book in the display window, the title of which concerns me fleetingly, but the content of which could hardly interest me. The second experience had a high degree of psychological value: I talked enthusiastically with my friend, the eye specialist, for probably an hour, made suggestions to him, which must have affected us both deeply and awakened memories in me, which made me aware of many different kinds of disturbances deep within me. What is more, this conversation was broken off without being completed, because acquaintances joined us. What relationship do these two impressions from the day before have to each other and to the dream which took place during the night?

In the dream content I can find only an allusion to the trivial impression and can therefore confirm that in a dream there is a preference for including trivial things from life in its content. But in the interpretation of a dream on the other hand, every-thing leads to the important experience which is rightfully the stimulus. If I assess the meaning of the dream, in the only correct way, according to the latent content brought to light by the analysis, then I have suddenly arrived at a new and import-ant insight. I see the puzzling assumption, that the dream only concerns itself with the worthless fragments of daily life, dissolve, and I must also refute the assertion that one's inner life while awake does not continue into the dreaming state so that a dream wastes its mental activity on silly things. The opposite is true: what has occupied us in the daytime also dom-inates our dream thoughts, and we take the trouble to dream about only those matters which had given us cause for thought during the day.

The obvious explanation for the fact that I nevertheless dream about the trivial impression of the day, while the one which is rightfully the stimulus has caused me to dream, is probably that here again the phenomenon of dream distortion is evident, which we have previously traced to a force in the psyche which imposes censorship. The memory of the monograph about the cyclamen genus is here used as if it were an *allusion* to the conversation with the friend, just as in the dream of the prevented dinner[24] the mentioning of the lady friend is represented by the allusion to 'smoked salmon'. The question is only, by what links the impression of the monograph can function as an allusion to the conversation with the eye specialist, as such a connection is not immediately apparent. In the example of the prevented dinner the connection is provided from the outset: 'smoked salmon', as the favourite food of the lady friend, can be readily seen to belong to the range of images which the figure of the lady friend can stimulate in the sleeping woman. In our new example it concerns two separate impressions, which at first have nothing in common, except that they occur on the same day. I notice the monograph during the morning, and I have the discussion in the evening. The answer which the analysis provides is as follows: such connections which are not at first available between the two impressions are developed subsequently between the image contained in the one and the image contained in the other. I have already emphasised the relevant links in writing the analysis. The only idea that could refer to the image of the monograph on the cyclamen, without any influence from elsewhere, would be that this is my wife's favourite flower, except perhaps also the memory of Frau L.'s missing bouquet. I do not believe that these hidden thoughts would have sufficed to provoke a dream. As it says in *Hamlet*:

> *There needs no ghost, my lord, come from the grave*
> *To tell us this*[25]

But behold! In the analysis I am reminded that the man who disturbed our conversation was called *Gärtner*, and that I found his wife to be *blooming*[26] with health. Indeed I recall now belatedly, that one of my patients, who bears the beautiful name of *Flora*, was for a while at the centre of our conversation. It must have happened that the combination of the two experiences of the day, the trivial and the stimulating ones, was conducted via these links from the botanical range of images. Then further connections occurred, those with cocaine, which can rightly mediate between the figure of Dr Königstein and a botanical monograph which I have written, and they strengthened this fusion of both ranges of images into one, so that now an item from the first experience could be employed as an allusion to the second.

I am prepared for the fact that this elucidation will be challenged as being arbitrary or artificial. What would have happened if Professor Gärtner and his wife, who was blooming with health, had not joined us, if the patient who was discussed was not called *Flora* but *Anna*? And yet there is a simple answer. If these thought connections had not arisen, then probably others would have been selected. It is so easy to produce such connections, as can be proved by those jokes and puzzles in the form of questions with which we brighten our days. The sphere of influence of wit is unlimited. To go one step further: if no sufficiently productive mediating connections could have been created, then the dream would have turned out differently. Another trivial impression of the day, hordes of which assail us and are forgotten by us, would have taken the place of the monograph for the dream, and would have established some connection with the content of the conversation and represented it in the dream. As no other impression except that of the monograph suffered this fate, then it must have been the most suitable one for making the link. There is never any need to be surprised, as was Lessing's character Hänschen Schlau, 'that only the rich people in the world possess the most gold'.[27]

Letter to Fritz Wittels, 15 August, 1924

Semmering, Villa Schüler, 15 August, 1924

Dear Doctor,

I have received[28] today the English translation of your book about me and leafed through it a little. This is the occasion of my writing to you…

… A biographer should at least have the intention of being as conscientious as a translator. As the proverb has it: *traduttore – traditore!*[29] I realise, that this was made especially more difficult for you by the circumstances. Thus it comes about that omissions arise, which show an affair in a false light, do an injustice directly to something, and similar things.

For example in the cocaine affair, to which you attach such great importance, for a reason of which I am not aware. The whole analogy with Brücke's discovery about the eye evaporates when one takes further into account something you do not know (or rather could have known about?): that I suspected it would probably be possible to apply it to the eye, but for personal reasons (to set off on a trip) I had to terminate the work and hand over the task of testing the substance on the eye directly to my friend Königstein. When I came back, he had made a bad job of it, and then given it up, and another, Koller, had become the discoverer.

The reader would also gain a different impression of my attitude to Koller's discovery, if he learned something, which of course you could not know, that it was Königstein – and *he* it was who was then so disappointed to have missed winning his laurels – who asserted his claim to be recognised as co-discoverer, and that both then named Julius Wagner *and myself* as arbitrators. I believe that it was then the honourable thing for us both to do, to take the side of the opposing party. Wagner, who was Königstein's spokesman, was in favour of recognising Königstein's claim, while I ascribed the honour completely to Koller alone. I no longer remember what compromise formula we agreed on…

… I greet you with the respect, which is proper towards you, in your superior position as biographer and with some of the old sympathy

Yours, Freud

From '*An Autobiographical Study*', 1925

I can go back at this point and relate that it was my wife's fault that I did not become famous in those days of my youth. In 1884 a remote but profound interest had induced me to have the Merck company send me some of the alkaloid cocaine, which was little known at the time, and to study its physiological effects. In the middle of this work the chance presented itself of going on a trip, to see my fiancée again, from whom I had been separated for two years. I finished my investigation into cocaine quickly and included in my publication the prediction that soon other applications for the substance would present themselves. And I suggested to my friend, the eye specialist L. Königstein, that he should investigate to what extent the anaesthetising properties of cocaine could be employed in treating diseased eyes. When I came back from holiday, I found that not he but another friend, Karl Koller (who is now in New York), whom I had also told about cocaine, had carried out the decisive experiments on animal eyes and had demonstrated them at the Conference of Ophthalmologists in Heidelberg. Koller is therefore rightfully regarded as the discoverer of the use of cocaine as a local anaesthetic, which has become so important for small-scale surgery; but I did not hold against my wife what I omitted to do at that time.[30]

Notes

1. The German word used here is 'Psyche', which is an important concept in Freud's theory of the mind and cannot be explained adequately here. It embraces both the emotional and cogitative functions of the mind. Freud sometimes uses the adjectival form, 'psychisch', which should not be confused with the popular connotations of the English word 'psychic', which has associations with the supernatural. The implications vary in Freud's own usage, so the present translator has translated it variously as 'psychological' and 'mental', with only occasional renderings as 'psychic', where the word should only be understood as meaning 'relating to Freud's concept of the psyche'.

2. 'Sopore beato' means 'blissful slumber'.

3. The term 'lebendige Kraft' (literally 'living energy') is a rendering by Freud of the Latin 'vis vitalis'. It would be rendered nowadays simply by 'energy'.

4. Freud is referring here to his treatment of his friend Ernst von Fleischl-Marxow.

5. The German expression which I have rendered as 'cranial nerve disorders' is 'Vagusneurosen'. It is worth noting that this is a pre-psychoanalytic use of the word 'Neurose' (neurosis) and implies here no more than a disorder of the nervous system.

6. This can be translated as 'the best possible way of tensing the vocal chords'.

7. Later, Freud was to distance himself from this recommendation to use subcutaneous injections.

8. This is Freud's strongest recommendation to apply cocaine subcutaneously by injection. He was later to retract this statement completely.

9. An 'at home event' or 'open house'.

10. In the nineteenth century the term 'idiosyncrasy' (in German 'Idiosynkrasie') came to be used to refer to individual differences in reactions to outer stimuli, especially to the effects of medication. A distinction was further made between innate and acquired idiosyncrasies.

11. 1 grain = approx. 0.065 grams.

12. The date given by Freud is an error repeated in all subsequent German editions of the work. Freud's first study of cocaine appeared in 1884.

13. 'Dr M.' clearly refers to Theodor Meynert who was head of the psychiatric clinic in which Freud was working.

14. There is some ambiguity here as the German verb 'erliegen' can mean 'succumb to' but is also often used to imply 'dying from' an illness.

15. These are both characters in a once very popular novel written by Fritz Reuter in the dialect of Mecklenburg, with the title *Ut mine Stromtid* (1862–4).

16. In German the first and last two syllables of each word sound the same: '<u>Dy</u>sen<u>terie</u>' and '<u>Diph</u><u>therie</u>'.

17. The friend was Wilhelm Fliess, biologist and nose and throat specialist in Berlin, and also a close friend who had a great influence on Freud while he was working on *The Interpretation of Dreams*. He is referred to anonymously many times in the work.

18. These aspects of the dream are analysed in another part of *The Interpretation of Dreams*, but in a way which is not relevant to a consideration of Freud's views on cocaine.

19. Freud is here making an association which is possible in both English and German. Germans also call someone who reads a lot a 'bookworm' ('Bücherwurm').

20. In his description of the dream earlier, Freud does not refer to the plate as 'folded', so it seems to be an illustration, probably larger than the page format, which folds out.

21. The German verb used here ('zerpflücken') has clear associations with 'picking' flowers, but in a destructive way.

22. 'Blatt für Blatt' in German. The word 'Blatt' is the normal word for 'leaf' in German but it is also the normal word for 'page', and not just metaphorical or poetic usage, as is the case with the word 'leaf'.

23. Freud does not draw attention to the fact here, but the word for 'favourite thing' ('Liebhaberei') has the root 'Liebhaber' which means both 'enthusiast' and 'lover'.

24. This refers to another dream analysed at length by Freud in *The Interpretation of Dreams*.

25. From Horatio's speech in William Shakespeare's *Hamlet*, Act I, Scene 5.

26. The name 'Gärtner' means of course 'gardener' and the word 'blühend' ('blooming') also has horticultural associations.

27. From one of the epigrams by G.E. Lessing (1729–81).

28. Freud actually wrote 'gelesen' ('read') but this does not make sense in the light of his subsequent remark that he had only 'leafed through it a little'.

29. 'traduttore – traditore' (Italian) means 'to translate is to betray'.

30. When Freud was preparing the text of *An Autobiographical Study* for a second edition in 1924, he changed the phrase in the last sentence, 'what I omitted to do at that time' ('mein damaliges Versäumnis'), to 'the disturbance at that time' ('die damalige Störung'). Some critics have suggested that Freud was thereby trying to shift the blame entirely onto Martha for the fact that he did not become known as the discoverer of the local anaesthetic properties of cocaine, but it is also just as likely that he wanted to make it clear that it was he who had disturbed his own work.

Select bibliography

Only those works are listed which are sources for the texts included or are referred to in the translator's Introduction and endnotes. A detailed bibliography on works relating to Freud's studies of cocaine can be found in Hirschmüller's edition of the *Schriften über Kokain*.

Sigmund Freud, *Briefe 1873–1939*, edited by Ernst and Lucie Freud, S. Fischer Verlag, Frankfurt-am-Main, 2nd edition, 1968.

Sigmund Freud, *Cocaine Papers*, edited with an introduction by Robert Byck, with notes by Anna Freud, New American Library, 1974.

Sigmund Freud, *Schriften über Kokain*, edited with an introduction by Albrecht Hirschmüller, S. Fischer Verlag, Frankfurt-am-Main, 3rd edition, 2004.

Sigmund Freud, *Studienausgabe*, in 10 volumes with additional unnumbered volume, and *Konkordanz und Gesamtbibliographie*, S. Fischer Verlag, Frankfurt-am-Main, 1969–75.

Jürgen von Scheidt, 'Sigmund Freud und das Kokain', in *Psyche*, XXVII, pp. 385–430, 1973.

Peter J. Swales, 'Freud, Cocaine, and Sexual Chemistry. The Role of Cocaine in Freud's Conception of the Libido.' Privately printed, and reprinted in *Sigmund Freud. Critical Assessments*, edited by Laurence Spurling, vol 1, pp. 273–302, Routledge, London and New York, 1989.

Biographical note

Sigmund Freud was born in a Moravian town (now situated in the Czech Republic) on 6 May 1856. The son of a wool merchant and the eldest of eight siblings, Freud moved with his family to Vienna following the economic crisis of 1857. Freud studied medicine at the University of Vienna and, in 1885, travelled to Paris to undertake a fellowship under renowned neurologist Jean-Martin Charcot. In 1886, Freud opened his own medical practice and married Martha Bernays. Specialising in neurology, Freud pioneered the 'talking cure' as a means of unlocking repressed emotions – this work is now widely seen as the basis of psychoanalysis. Freud is also best remembered for his work on the unconscious, the effect of childhood on personality and dream analysis, though these made up only a small part of his areas of research.

In June 1938, Freud left Nazi Germany and took refuge in London, settling in Hampstead. In September 1939, suffering from cancer and in severe pain, Freud persuaded his friend Max Schur to help him commit suicide: he died as a result of morphine overdose on 23 September 1939.

Dr David Carter has taught at St Andrews and Southampton universities in the UK and has been Professor of Communicative English at Yonsei University, Seoul. His Ph.D. was on Freud's theories of creativity and aesthetics and he has taught on Freud and Jung. He has published on psychoanalysis, literature, drama, film history and applied linguistics, and is also a freelance journalist and translator. He has published books on the Belgian author Georges Simenon and Literary Theory, as well as in the field of film studies, the most recent being *East Asian Cinema* and *The Western*. For Hesperus he has written *Brief Lives: Honoré de Balzac* and translated Balzac's 'Sarrasine', Georges Simenon's *Three Crimes*, and Klaus Mann's *Alexander*.